A Taste of the Good Life

A Taste of the Good Life
from the Heart of Tennessee

*Additional copies of
A Taste of the Good Life,
and other information on
Saint Thomas programs,
may be obtained by
calling 1-800-222-3541,
or by writing to Saint
Thomas Heart Institute,
4220 Harding Road,
Nashville, Tennessee
37205.*

Executive Editor: Nancy Becker
Project Manager: Tom Anderson
Recipe and Menu Editor: Kitty Fawaz, R.D., L.D.N.
Contributing Editor: Barbara Smith, R.N.
Essayist: Mark Lee Taylor
Typist: Connie Rafalowski
Photography: Chris Kelly Photography
Vintage Photography: Ophelia Paine,
Metropolitan Historical Commission

This cookbook is a collection of favorite recipes,
which are not necessarily original recipes.

Published by Saint Thomas Hospital

Copyright© Saint Thomas Hospital
4220 Harding Road
Nashville, Tennessee 37205

ISBN: 0-9655243-0-2

Edited, Designed, and Manufactured by
FRP™
P.O. Box 305142
Nashville, Tennessee 37230
1-800-358-0560

Editorial Project Manager: Debbie Van Mol
Editor: Georgia Brazil
Cover and Book Design: Barbara Ball
Typographer: Sara Anglin

Manufactured in the United States
First Printing: 1996   7,500 copies

CONTENTS

At the Heart of This Book

Nashville—a city rich in history, music and Southern charm. It's the heart of Tennessee, geographically and figuratively. It's also home of the meat and three. (That's Southern shorthand for meat and three vegetables, for those of us not fortunate enough to have been born in the land of country ham and red-eye gravy.)

From church suppers to summertime picnics, good cooking is a part of Nashville's heritage. We are loath to part with tradition, even though we know now that some of our most cherished favorites are not exactly good for us.

While living a heart-healthy lifestyle is something most of us aspire to, it's not always what we practice when it comes to eating. Flavorful cooking may even seem incompatible with foods that are good for the heart.

Not so. That's how we came to compile this book. For years we've been showing cardiac rehabilitation patients there's a lot of good eating that's good for you, too. People who want to eat a low-fat, low-cholesterol diet can still enjoy many traditional Southern favorites, with just a few changes here and there. Plus, once you learn the basic substitutions, you'll even be able to modify many of your own favorites.

All of our recipes have been carefully analyzed to make sure they fall within the guidelines of low-fat, low-cholesterol cooking. At the end of each recipe, we've given you the nutritional information you need to keep track of your intake of fat, calories and sodium. In some cases, we've also given you an analysis of the original recipe, so you can feel even better about the fat and calories you're not eating. But best of all, these recipes have been taste-tested by people who love home cooking.

Along with the recipes, you'll find practical ideas to use as you work toward a healthier lifestyle. We hope you'll enjoy reading them and incorporate some of them into your own routine. We also hope you'll enjoy the photographs that contrast a Nashville of the past with its vibrant present.

All proceeds from the sale of this book will be used to further Saint Thomas Heart Institute cardiac research and education so that more people can benefit from the joys of living a heart-healthy lifestyle.

Happy, healthy eating!

Nancy Becker

Nancy Becker
Saint Thomas Heart Institute

ABOUT THE SAINT THOMAS
HEART INSTITUTE

A nationally respected leader in cardiac care, the Saint Thomas Heart Institute is one of the five largest cardiac programs in the country. Its mission is to provide high-quality, cost-effective, compassionate cardiac care by reducing the incidence and severity of cardiovascular disease through education and preventive health measures, and by providing the best value in cardiac care through exceptional quality and the lowest possible cost.

The Heart Institute is affiliated with Nashville's Saint Thomas Hospital, which was founded by the Daughters of Charity in 1898. Its long list of "firsts" includes the first coronary artery bypass surgery in Tennessee, the first heart transplant in Tennessee, and the first cardiac rehabilitation program in the nation to conduct real-time monitored exercise sessions with out-of-town patients via telephone.

Over the past three decades, the cardiac care team at Saint Thomas has performed more than 110,000 catheterizations, more than 33,000 open heart surgeries, more than 11,000 angioplasties, and more than 125 heart transplants.

The Heart Institute's programs in prevention and rehabilitation are second to none. Its rehabilitation program is one of the country's largest. Education and physical conditioning are cornerstones of the rehabilitation program, with innovative services that focus on risk reduction through behavior modification. Prevention programs include exercise classes, nutrition education and cooking classes, stress management, smoking cessation, lipid profiling, and weight management.

Working with patients, families, employers, and the public, the Saint Thomas Heart Institute is committed not just to healing the sick, but to the encouragement of healthy bodies, minds, and spirits.

THEN AND NOW

Times have changed drastically since June Cleaver, one of television's most famous mothers, was in charge of America's kitchen. The room that was once considered "off limits" for anyone except women is now open to everyone. The personal time issues in every household make it imperative that everyone know how to prepare healthy food.

Mrs. Cleaver's shirtwaist dress and pearls aren't the only things that have changed in the kitchen. We know a whole lot more about what's good for us, and what is not. Sometimes that's difficult to live with, because many of our favorites are not necessarily the best nutritional choices. Just think about the occasions that involve fat-laden and cholesterol-loaded food: Thanksgiving Dinner, A Southern-Style Fried Chicken Dinner, A Summer Fish Fry, or A Country Breakfast.

Staying on the nutritional "straight-and-narrow" must be more difficult in the South than anywhere else, because it seems one cannot participate in *any* activity without food being offered. This makes it tricky for people who *must* watch what they eat. With more than two-thirds of the United States marching into middle age, the reality is that most of us should be making behavioral changes in our eating habits. Use these "now" suggestions to make excess fat and calories "a blast from the past" and ensure a healthier and fitter future.

Saint Thomas Hospital, built in 1902 on Hayes Street, Nashville. Inset: The current Saint Thomas Hospital campus at 4220 Harding Road, Nashville.

THEN

COUNTRY BREAKFAST

Garlic Cheese Grits ♦ Scrambled Eggs
Country Ham ♦ Red-Eye Gravy
Buttermilk Biscuits ♦ Molasses ♦ Honey
Assorted Jams and Jellies
Orange Juice

CALORIES: 1122; TOTAL FAT: 73 g; CHOLESTEROL: 590 mg; SODIUM: 3280 mg
CALORIES FROM FAT: 59%

NOW

COUNTRY BREAKFAST

Spicy Grits Casserole *page 11*
Tomato Basil Cheese Omelet *page 12*
Pan-Broiled Pork Tenderloin ♦ Buttermilk Biscuits *page 13*
Warm Fruit Compote *page 14* ♦ Assorted Jams and Jellies
Honey ♦ Molasses ♦ Orange Juice

CALORIES: 666; TOTAL FAT: 9 g; CHOLESTEROL: 63 mg; SODIUM: 959 mg
CALORIES FROM FAT: 12%

Spicy Grits Casserole

2¼ cups water
¼ teaspoon salt
¾ cup quick-cooking grits
2 ounces low-fat Cheddar cheese, shredded
1 (4-ounce) can chopped green chiles, drained
1 (2-ounce) jar diced pimento, drained
1 clove of garlic, crushed
¼ teaspoon hot sauce
¼ cup frozen egg substitute, thawed

Bring the water and salt to a boil in a medium saucepan. Stir in the grits; reduce heat. Simmer, covered, for 5 minutes or until thickened, stirring occasionally. Remove from heat. Add the cheese, chiles, pimento, garlic and hot sauce, stirring until the cheese melts. Stir ¼ of the hot grits mixture gradually into the egg substitute in a medium bowl. Add the egg substitute mixture to the grits, stirring constantly. Spoon into a 1-quart baking dish sprayed with nonstick cooking spray. Bake at 350 degrees for 30 minutes or until set. **Yield:** 6 servings.

Per Serving:
Calories: 108; Carbohydrate: 17 g; Protein: 6 g; Total Fat: 2 g;
Cholesterol: 6 mg; Sodium: 282 mg; Fiber: trace;
Calories from Fat: 18%

Then and Now

Prepare your own egg substitute by beating 3 egg whites lightly. Add a mixture of 2 tablespoons skim milk and 1 tablespoon nonfat dry milk powder and beat until blended. Stir in ½ teaspoon vegetable oil. Blend in 1 or 2 drops of yellow food coloring if desired. Egg substitute may be scrambled, made into omelets, used to make French toast, or used as a substitute for whole eggs in many recipes.

TOMATO BASIL CHEESE OMELET

½ cup egg substitute
1 ounce fat-free mozzarella cheese, shredded
¼ cup chopped fresh tomato
1 tablespoon chopped fresh basil

Spray a skillet with nonstick cooking spray. Heat the skillet over medium-high heat until hot. Pour the egg substitute into the prepared skillet, tilting the skillet to cover the bottom evenly. Cook until almost set; turn the omelet. Sprinkle with the cheese, tomato and basil; fold in half. Cook until the cheese melts. Serve immediately. **Yield:** 1 serving.

PER SERVING:
CALORIES: 106; CARBOHYDRATE: 4.2 g; PROTEIN: 17.1 g; TOTAL FAT: 0 g; CHOLESTEROL: <5 mg; SODIUM: 350 mg; FIBER: trace; CALORIES FROM FAT: 0%

Buttermilk Biscuits

2 cups flour
2 teaspoons baking powder
½ teaspoon baking soda
¼ teaspoon salt
¼ cup reduced-calorie margarine
¾ cup plus 1 tablespoon low-fat buttermilk
1½ teaspoons flour

Combine 2 cups flour, baking powder, baking soda and salt in a medium bowl and mix well. Cut in the margarine with a pastry blender until crumbly. Add the buttermilk, stirring just until moistened. Sprinkle 1½ teaspoons flour evenly over work surface. Knead the dough 5 or 6 times on the floured surface. Roll the dough ½ inch thick; cut with a 2½-inch biscuit cutter. Arrange on a baking sheet sprayed with nonstick cooking spray. Bake at 425 degrees for 10 to 12 minutes or until golden brown. **Yield:** 8 (1-biscuit) servings.

Per Serving:
Calories: 157; Carbohydrate: 26 g; Protein: 4 g; Total Fat: 4 g;
Cholesterol: 1 mg; Sodium: 282 mg; Fiber: trace;
Calories from Fat: 23%

Read labels. Low-fat means 3 grams or less per serving. Low-sodium means less than 140 milligrams per serving. Low-cholesterol means less than 20 milligrams per serving. Low-calorie means less than 40 calories per serving.

Then and Now

Warm Fruit Compote

8 ounces mixed seasonal fresh fruit, sliced
4 ounces all fruit preserves (All-Fruit, Sorrel Ridge or
Simply Fruit)
4 ounces peach or apricot nectar
2 tablespoons orange zest

Combine the fruit, fruit preserves, peach nectar and orange zest in a saucepan and mix well. Cook over low heat just until warm, stirring occasionally; do not boil. Serve immediately. Fresh berries, peaches, nectarines, apricots, bananas, mangoes, papayas, pineapples and cherries would all be appropriate in this compote. Let the season act as the guide, and select very ripe fruits that will sweeten the sauce. If the sauce is too sweet, add a few drops of lemon juice, lime juice or orange juice. **Yield:** 8 servings.

PER SERVING:
CALORIES: 80; CARBOHYDRATE: 15 g; PROTEIN: 1 g; TOTAL FAT: trace;
CHOLESTEROL: 0 mg; SODIUM: 5 mg; FIBER: trace;
CALORIES FROM FAT: 0%

THEN AND NOW

THEN

Thanksgiving Dinner

Pumpkin Bread with Cream Cheese
Cranberry Salad ♦ Oven-Roasted Turkey
Turkey Gravy ♦ Corn Bread Dressing
Mashed Potatoes ♦ Country Green Beans
Dinner Rolls ♦ Pumpkin Pie

CALORIES: 1825; TOTAL FAT: 100 g; CHOLESTEROL: 306 mg; SODIUM: 3173 mg
CALORIES FROM FAT: 50%

Now

Thanksgiving Dinner

Pumpkin Bread with Nonfat Cream Cheese *page 16*
Cranberry Salad *page 17* ♦ Oven-Roasted Turkey *page 18*
Turkey Gravy *page 18* ♦ Low-Fat Corn Bread Dressing *page 19*
Mashed Potatoes *page 20* ♦ Country Green Beans *page 20*
Yogurt Dinner Rolls *page 21* ♦ Light Crunchy Crust Pumpkin Pie *page 22*

CALORIES: 1082; TOTAL FAT: 16 g; CHOLESTEROL: 77 mg; SODIUM: 1034 mg
CALORIES FROM FAT: 13%

Pumpkin Bread

3½ cups flour
2 teaspoons baking soda
1½ teaspoons pumpkin pie spice
½ teaspoon baking powder
½ teaspoon salt
¼ teaspoon cinnamon
2½ cups sugar
1 cup egg substitute
⅔ cup water
⅓ cup canola oil
1 (16-ounce) can pumpkin

Spray two 5x9-inch loaf pans with nonstick cooking spray. Combine the flour, baking soda, pumpkin pie spice, baking powder, salt and cinnamon in a bowl and mix well. Beat the sugar and egg substitute in a large mixer bowl until creamy. Add the dry ingredients, water, oil and pumpkin. Beat until blended, scraping the bowl occasionally. Spoon evenly into the prepared loaf pans. Bake at 325 degrees for 65 to 70 minutes or until loaves test done. Cool in pans on a wire rack. Invert onto wire rack. Serve with nonfat cream cheese. **Yield:** 36 (½-inch slice) servings.

Per Serving:
Calories: 123; Carbohydrate: 24 g; Protein: 1.5 g; Total Fat: 2 g;
Cholesterol: 0 mg; Sodium: 94 mg; Fiber: trace;
Calories from Fat: 18%

Then and Now

CRANBERRY SALAD

12 ounces fresh cranberries, ground
2 cups seedless red grape halves
½ cup chopped walnuts
1½ cups sugar
1 (16-ounce) can juice-pack crushed pineapple
8 ounces light whipped topping

Combine the cranberries, grape halves and walnuts in a bowl and mix gently. Add the sugar and pineapple, stirring until mixed. Marinate, covered, in the refrigerator for 8 to 10 hours. Stir in the whipped topping just before serving. Spoon into a serving bowl. **Yield:** 20 servings.

PER SERVING:
CALORIES: 126; CARBOHYDRATE: 24 g; PROTEIN: 0.6 g; TOTAL FAT: 3.3 g;
CHOLESTEROL: 0 mg; SODIUM: 1 mg; FIBER: 0.4 g;
CALORIES FROM FAT: 24%

Use fresh fruit whenever possible. If canned must be used, select varieties packed in water or fruit juices. Avoid heavy syrups.

THEN AND NOW

Oven-Roasted Turkey

1 turkey breast
Chopped fresh sage, parsley, thyme
and/or rosemary to taste

Rinse the turkey and pat dry. Remove the skin. Spray all sides of the turkey with butter-flavor nonstick cooking spray. Rub with fresh herbs. Wrap the turkey in cheesecloth; place in a cooking bag. Bake at 375 degrees until meat thermometer registers 170 degrees. **Yield:** Variable.

Per 3-Ounce Serving:
Calories: 135; Carbohydrate: 0 g; Protein: 21 g; Total Fat: 2 g;
Cholesterol: 60 mg; Sodium: 59 mg; Fiber: trace;
Calories from Fat: 15%

Turkey Gravy

2 cups low-fat low-sodium turkey broth
3 tablespoons cornstarch
¼ cup water

Skim the turkey broth to remove fat. Pour into a saucepan. Bring to a boil; reduce heat. Stir in a mixture of the cornstarch and water. Cook until of the desired consistency, stirring constantly. Remove from heat. Serve immediately. **Yield:** 8 (¼ -cup) servings.

Per Serving:
Calories: 16; Carbohydrate: 3 g; Protein: 1 g; Total Fat: trace;
Cholesterol: 0 mg; Sodium: 12 mg; Fiber: trace;
Calories from Fat: 11%

Then and Now

Low-Fat Corn Bread Dressing

½ cup finely chopped celery
½ cup chopped onion
1 tablespoon finely chopped fresh parsley
1½ teaspoons ground sage
2¾ cups corn bread stuffing
1 to 1½ cups chicken broth, skimmed

Spray a medium skillet lightly with nonstick cooking spray. Add the celery and onion to the prepared skillet. Cook over medium heat until the vegetables are tender, stirring constantly. Stir in the parsley and sage. Combine the corn bread stuffing and celery mixture in a bowl and mix well. Add the chicken broth, stirring just until moistened. Spoon into a 1½- to 2-quart baking dish sprayed lightly with nonstick cooking spray. Bake at 350 degrees for 30 to 40 minutes or until heated through. For Chestnut Corn Bread Dressing add ½ cup chopped boiled Chinese chestnuts to the dressing and bake as directed. **Yield:** 4 servings.

Per Serving:
Calories: 174; Carbohydrate: 33 g; Protein: 5 g; Total Fat: 2 g;
Cholesterol: 0 mg; Sodium: 475 mg; Fiber: trace;
Calories from Fat: 11%

Sometimes it's too hot or humid to exercise. If conditions are going to be bad, exercise during the cool parts of the day, or visit your local mall for a quick-paced walk.

Then and Now

Mashed Potatoes

6 potatoes, peeled ♦ 1 cup skim milk
1 teaspoon minced garlic ♦ Pepper to taste
¼ cup grated fat-free Parmesan cheese, or to taste

Combine the potatoes with enough water to cover in a saucepan. Cook until tender. Drain, reserving 1 cup of the liquid. Heat the skim milk in a saucepan until very warm. Beat the potatoes in a mixer bowl until smooth. Add 3 sprays of butter-flavor nonstick cooking spray, garlic and pepper. Beat until blended, scraping the bowl occasionally. Add the warm skim milk and reserved potato liquid until of the desired consistency, beating until blended. Beat in the cheese until smooth. **Yield:** 6 servings.

Per Serving:
Calories: 118; Carbohydrate: 24 g; Protein: 6 g; Total Fat: trace;
Cholesterol: 1 mg; Sodium: 93 mg; Fiber: trace;
Calories from Fat: 2%

Country Green Beans

1 pound fresh green beans
1 teaspoon low-sodium beef bouillon
1 teaspoon Worcestershire sauce
1 onion, sliced ♦ 1 teaspoon olive oil
Liquid smoke (optional)

Trim the beans; remove the strings. Combine the beans, bouillon, Worcestershire sauce, onion, olive oil and liquid smoke in a saucepan. Add enough water to cover. Cook, covered, until the beans are tender and the liquid is absorbed, stirring occasionally. **Yield:** 4 servings.

Per Serving:
Calories: 44; Carbohydrate: 7 g; Protein: 1 g; Total Fat: 1 g;
Cholesterol: 0 mg; Sodium: 17 mg; Fiber: trace;
Calories from Fat: 28%

Then and Now

Yogurt Dinner Rolls

¼ cup lukewarm water
2 tablespoons sugar
1 envelope dry yeast
1 cup nonfat plain yogurt
2 tablespoons melted margarine
1 egg, lightly beaten
2 tablespoons grated onion
2 teaspoons basil
1 teaspoon leaf oregano
¾ cup all-purpose flour
¾ cup whole wheat flour
½ teaspoon salt
½ cup all-purpose flour
¾ cup whole wheat flour

Combine the lukewarm water, sugar and yeast in a bowl and mix well. Let stand for 5 minutes or until bubbly. Stir in the yogurt, margarine, egg, onion, basil and oregano. Combine ¾ cup all-purpose flour, ¾ cup whole wheat flour and salt in a mixer bowl and mix well. Add the yeast mixture. Beat at low speed for 30 seconds. Beat at high speed for 3 minutes, scraping the bowl occasionally. Stir in ½ cup all-purpose flour and ¾ cup whole wheat flour; dough will be moist and sticky. Place in a bowl sprayed with nonstick cooking spray, turning to coat the dough surface. Let rise, covered with a tea towel, for 1½ hours. Punch the dough down. Shape into 18 balls. Arrange the dough balls in a 9x13-inch baking pan sprayed with nonstick cooking spray. Let rise for 40 minutes. Bake at 400 degrees for 15 minutes. **Yield:** 18 (1-roll) servings.

Per Serving:
Calories: 93; Carbohydrate: 16 g; Protein: 3 g; Total Fat: 2 g;
Cholesterol: 15 mg; Sodium: 89 mg; Fiber: trace;
Calories from Fat: 19%

Then and Now

LIGHT CRUNCHY CRUST PUMPKIN PIE

Crust
1¼ cups quick-cooking oats
⅓ cup packed brown sugar
¼ cup flour
2 tablespoons melted margarine
2 tablespoons egg substitute

Filling
1 (14-ounce) can fat-free sweetened condensed milk
1⅓ cups mashed pumpkin
½ cup egg substitute
1 teaspoon cinnamon
½ teaspoon ginger ♦ ⅛ teaspoon nutmeg
¼ teaspoon allspice

For the crust, combine the oats, brown sugar and flour in a bowl and mix well. Add the margarine and 2 tablespoons egg substitute, stirring until mixed. Pat mixture over bottom and up side of a 9-inch pie plate sprayed with nonstick cooking spray.

For the filling, combine the condensed milk, pumpkin, ½ cup egg substitute, cinnamon, ginger, nutmeg and allspice in a mixer bowl, beating until blended; do not overmix. Pour into the prepared pie plate. Bake at 400 degrees for 15 minutes; reduce oven temperature to 350 degrees. Bake for 20 to 30 minutes longer or until set. Let stand until cool. Chill until serving time. **Yield:** 8 servings.

PER SERVING:
CALORIES: 280; CARBOHYDRATE: 54 g; PROTEIN: 9 g; TOTAL FAT: 3.5 g;
CHOLESTEROL: trace; SODIUM: 126 mg; FIBER: trace;
CALORIES FROM FAT: 11%

THEN AND NOW

THEN

SOUTHERN FRIED CHICKEN DINNER

Fried Chicken
Fried Green Tomatoes
Southern-Style White Beans
Cracklin' Corn Bread
Granny's Chocolate Mocha Cake

CALORIES: 1826; TOTAL FAT: 115 g; CHOLESTEROL: 407 mg; SODIUM: 1543 mg
CALORIES FROM FAT: 57%

NOW

SOUTHERN FRIED CHICKEN DINNER

Oven-Fried Chicken *page 24*
Oven-Fried Green Tomatoes *page 25*
White Beans *page 26*
Cracklin' Corn Bread *page 26*
Granny's Chocolate Mocha Cake *page 27*

CALORIES: 1084; TOTAL FAT: 10 g; CHOLESTEROL: 88 mg; SODIUM: 1310 mg
CALORIES FROM FAT: 8%

Oven-Fried Chicken

6 whole chicken breasts, split, skinned
3½ cups ice water
1 cup plain nonfat yogurt
1 cup Italian-seasoned bread crumbs
1 cup flour
1 tablespoon Old Bay seasoning
½ teaspoon garlic powder
½ teaspoon Creole seasoning or Cajun seasoning
½ teaspoon thyme
½ teaspoon basil
½ teaspoon oregano
⅛ teaspoon freshly ground black pepper
Cayenne to taste

Spray a baking sheet 3 times with nonstick cooking spray. Rinse the chicken. Place the chicken in the ice water in a bowl. Spoon the yogurt into a medium bowl. Combine the bread crumbs, flour, Old Bay seasoning, garlic powder, Creole seasoning, thyme, basil, oregano, black pepper and cayenne in a sealable plastic bag, shaking to mix. Remove 2 pieces of the chicken from the water; coat with the yogurt. Place the chicken in the plastic bag, shaking to coat. Arrange on the prepared baking sheet. Repeat the process with the remaining chicken. Spray the chicken lightly with nonstick cooking spray. Place the baking sheet on the bottom oven rack. Bake at 400 degrees for 1 hour, turning every 20 minutes to assure even browning.
Yield: 12 servings.

Per Serving:
Calories: 226; Carbohydrate: 15 g; Protein: 30 g; Total Fat: 3.6 g;
Cholesterol: 73 mg; Sodium: 312 mg; Fiber: 0 g;
Calories from Fat: 14%

Then and Now

Oven-Fried Green Tomatoes

2 egg whites
¼ cup water
2½ cups bread crumbs
¼ teaspoon pepper
6 green tomatoes, thickly sliced

Spray 2 baking sheets with nonstick cooking spray. Beat the egg whites and water in a bowl. Combine the bread crumbs and pepper in a bowl and mix well. Dip the tomato slices in the egg white mixture; coat with the bread crumb mixture. Arrange on the prepared baking sheets. Spray the tomato slices lightly with nonstick cooking spray. Bake at 400 degrees for 25 to 30 minutes or until tender, crisp and light brown, turning occasionally. **Yield:** 6 servings.

PER SERVING:
CALORIES: 201; CARBOHYDRATE: 31 g; PROTEIN: 7 g; TOTAL FAT: 1 g;
CHOLESTEROL: 0 mg; SODIUM: 339 mg; FIBER: trace;
CALORIES FROM FAT: 7%

Do not use nonstick cooking spray near an open flame or a heat source. Read directions on the can, and follow directions carefully.

THEN AND NOW

White Beans

2 cups dried white beans ♦ 2 quarts water
1 onion, sliced (optional)
1 tablespoon low-sodium chicken bouillon granules
2 teaspoons olive oil ♦ ½ teaspoon beef bouillon granules
¼ teaspoon salt ♦ ⅛ teaspoon ginger ♦ ⅛ teaspoon red pepper

Sort and rinse the white beans. Combine with 2 quarts water in a bowl. Let stand for 8 to 10 hours. Drain and rinse. Place the beans in a 3-quart saucepan. Add enough water to cover by 1 inch. Bring to a boil; reduce heat. Skim off foam. Stir in the onion, chicken bouillon, olive oil, beef bouillon, salt, ginger and red pepper. Simmer, covered, over low heat for 1½ to 2 hours or until the beans are of the desired tenderness, stirring occasionally. **Yield:** 8 servings.

Per Serving:
Calories: 103; Carbohydrate: 22.4 g; Protein: 8 g; Total Fat: 3.4 g;
Cholesterol: 0 mg; Sodium: 150 mg; Fiber: trace;
Calories from Fat: 29%

Cracklin' Corn Bread

1 cup low-fat buttermilk ♦ ½ teaspoon baking soda
1 cup self-rising cornmeal ♦ ¼ cup flour
¼ cup whole kernel corn, drained ♦ 2 teaspoons canola oil

Spray an 8-inch cast-iron skillet with nonstick cooking spray. Heat the skillet at 450 degrees for 5 minutes. Mix the buttermilk and baking soda in a bowl. Add the cornmeal and flour, stirring until mixed. Stir in the corn and canola oil. Spoon into the prepared skillet. Bake at 450 degrees for 20 to 25 minutes or until golden brown. Remove from oven. Invert onto a serving plate. **Yield:** 8 servings.

Per Serving:
Calories: 75; Carbohydrate: 12.5 g; Protein: 2.3 g; Total Fat: 1.9 g;
Cholesterol: 1.1 mg; Sodium: 234 mg; Fiber: trace;
Calories from Fat: 23%

Granny's Chocolate Mocha Cake

Cake
2 cups flour ♦ 2 cups sugar ♦ 1 cup unsweetened baking cocoa
2 teaspoons baking soda ♦ 1 teaspoon baking powder
¼ teaspoon salt ♦ 1 cup skim milk
4 (2½-ounce) jars baby food puréed prunes ♦ 4 egg whites
1 cup cappuccino (prepared from mix) ♦ 2 teaspoons vanilla extract

Frosting
1½ cups packed light brown sugar ♦ 3 egg whites
¼ cup cappuccino (prepared from mix) ♦ 1 teaspoon cream of tartar
1 teaspoon vanilla extract

For the cake, sift the first 6 ingredients into a bowl and mix well. Combine the skim milk, prunes, 4 egg whites, 1 cup cappuccino and 2 teaspoons vanilla in a bowl and mix well. Add to the dry ingredients, stirring until blended. Spoon into two 9-inch round cake pans or a 9x13-inch cake pan sprayed with nonstick cooking spray. Bake at 350 degrees for 30 to 35 minutes or until the layers test done. Cool in the pans for 10 minutes. Invert onto a wire rack to cool completely. May substitute 2 teaspoons instant coffee granules dissolved in 1 cup boiling water, 1 cup strong coffee or 1 cup water for the cappuccino and egg substitute equivalent to 2 eggs for the egg whites.

For the frosting, bring water to a boil in the bottom of a double boiler; reduce heat to low. Combine the brown sugar, 3 egg whites, ¼ cup cappuccino and cream of tartar in the top of the double boiler. Beat with a mixer over simmering water for 5 to 7 minutes or until stiff peaks form. Remove from heat. Stir in 1 teaspoon vanilla. Beat for 3 minutes longer. May substitute 1 tablespoon instant coffee granules dissolved in ¼ cup boiling water or ¼ cup strong coffee for the cappuccino. Spread the frosting between the layers and over the top and side of the cake. **Yield:** 12 servings.

PER SERVING:
CALORIES: 512; CARBOHYDRATE: 83 g; PROTEIN: 7 g; TOTAL FAT: 1 g;
CHOLESTEROL: 0 mg; SODIUM: 291 mg; FIBER: trace;
CALORIES FROM FAT: 2%

Use baking cocoa in place of chocolate chips or baking squares of chocolate to reduce fat content.

THEN AND NOW

Then

SUMMER FISH FRY

Celery Seed Coleslaw
Fried Catfish
French Fries
Hush Puppies
Lemonade Cooler Pie

CALORIES: 1379; TOTAL FAT: 64 g; CHOLESTEROL: 131 mg; SODIUM: 1949 mg
CALORIES FROM FAT: 42%

Now

SUMMER FISH FRY

Celery Seed Coleslaw *page 29*
Oven-Fried Catfish *page 29*
Oven French Fries *page 30*
Baked Hush Puppies *page 30*
Lemonade Cooler Pie *page 31*

CALORIES: 490; TOTAL FAT: 11 g; CHOLESTEROL: 65 mg; SODIUM: 592 mg
CALORIES FROM FAT: 20%

CELERY SEED COLESLAW

3 cups finely shredded cabbage ♦ ⅓ cup vinegar, heated
1 teaspoon canola oil ♦ 2 tablespoons sugar
1 tablespoon finely chopped onion
1 tablespoon chopped pimento
½ teaspoon dry mustard ♦ ½ teaspoon salt
½ teaspoon celery seeds

Toss the cabbage, vinegar and canola oil in a bowl. Add the sugar, onion, pimento, dry mustard, salt and celery seeds and mix well. Chill, covered, until serving time. **Yield:** 6 servings.

PER SERVING:
CALORIES: 34; CARBOHYDRATE: 6.4 g; PROTEIN: 0.4 g; TOTAL FAT: 0.8 g;
CHOLESTEROL: 0 mg; SODIUM: 198 mg; FIBER: trace;
CALORIES FROM FAT: 23%

OVEN-FRIED CATFISH

4 (4-ounce) catfish fillets ♦ ½ teaspoon garlic powder
½ teaspoon lemon pepper ♦ 1 tablespoon blackening seasoning
¼ cup cornmeal ♦ 1 teaspoon thyme
1 teaspoon basil ♦ ½ teaspoon paprika

Spray a baking sheet 3 times with nonstick cooking spray. Sprinkle the fillets on both sides with the garlic powder, lemon pepper and blackening seasoning. Coat with a mixture of the cornmeal, thyme and basil. Arrange the fillets on the prepared baking sheet; sprinkle with the paprika. Spray each fillet lightly with nonstick cooking spray. Place the baking sheet on the bottom oven rack. Bake at 400 degrees for 20 minutes; reduce the oven temperature to 350 degrees. Bake for 5 minutes longer or until the fish flakes easily. **Yield:** 4 servings.

PER SERVING:
CALORIES: 163; CARBOHYDRATE: 7 g; PROTEIN: 21 g; TOTAL FAT: 4.8 g;
CHOLESTEROL: 65 mg; SODIUM: 304 mg; FIBER: trace;
CALORIES FROM FAT: 26%

THEN AND NOW

Oven French Fries

4 large unpeeled potatoes
2 tablespoons peanut oil or safflower oil

Cut the potatoes into ½-inch-wide strips. Place in a bowl of ice water. Chill, covered, for 1 to 2 hours. Drain and pat dry. Combine the potatoes and peanut oil in a bowl, tossing to coat. Arrange in a single layer in a shallow baking pan. Bake at 475 degrees for 30 to 35 minutes, turning occasionally. **Yield:** 8 servings.

PER SERVING:
CALORIES: 130; CARBOHYDRATE: 23 g; PROTEIN: 2 g; TOTAL FAT: 3 g;
CHOLESTEROL: 0 mg; SODIUM: 7 mg; FIBER: trace;
CALORIES FROM FAT: 20%

Baked Hush Puppies

⅔ cup cornmeal ◆ ½ cup minced onion
⅓ cup flour
1 teaspoon baking powder
¼ teaspoon salt ◆ ⅓ cup skim milk
¼ cup frozen egg substitute, thawed
1 tablespoon canola oil

Spray miniature muffin cups with nonstick cooking spray. Combine the cornmeal, onion, flour, baking powder and salt in a bowl and mix well. Make a well in the center of the mixture. Pour a mixture of the skim milk, egg substitute and canola oil into the well and stir just until moistened. Fill the prepared muffin cups ¾ full. Bake at 450 degrees for 12 to 15 minutes or until light brown. Remove hush puppies from muffin cups immediately. Serve warm.
Yield: 24 (1-hush puppy) servings.

PER SERVING:
CALORIES: 31; CARBOHYDRATE: 4.8 g; PROTEIN: 0.9 g; TOTAL FAT: 0.9 g;
CHOLESTEROL: 0 mg; SODIUM: 43 mg; FIBER: 0.3 g;
CALORIES FROM FAT: 26%

THEN AND NOW

LEMONADE COOLER PIE

½ to 1 cup graham cracker crumbs
2 tablespoons melted reduced-calorie margarine
4 cups frozen vanilla nonfat yogurt, softened
1 (12-ounce) can frozen lemonade concentrate

Combine the graham cracker crumbs and margarine in a bowl and mix well. Pat over the bottom and up the side of an 8- or 9-inch pie plate. Freeze for 5 minutes. Combine the yogurt and unthawed lemonade concentrate in a bowl and mix well. Spoon into the prepared pie plate. Freeze until serving time. **Yield:** 10 servings.

PER SERVING:
CALORIES: 132; CARBOHYDRATE: 41.7 g; PROTEIN: 2.8 g; TOTAL FAT: 1.5 g;
CHOLESTEROL: 0 mg; SODIUM: 40 mg; FIBER: trace;
CALORIES FROM FAT: 10%

When Gertrude Miller, 79 years young, started her exercise program she was able to walk 1.0 mile per hour for 5 minutes, and lift 1 pound in each hand over her head 5 times. Eight months later, Ms. Miller was able to walk 2.4 miles per hour for 30 minutes, and lift 12 pounds in each hand over her head 10 times . . . truly an inspirational woman.

THEN AND NOW

Celebrations

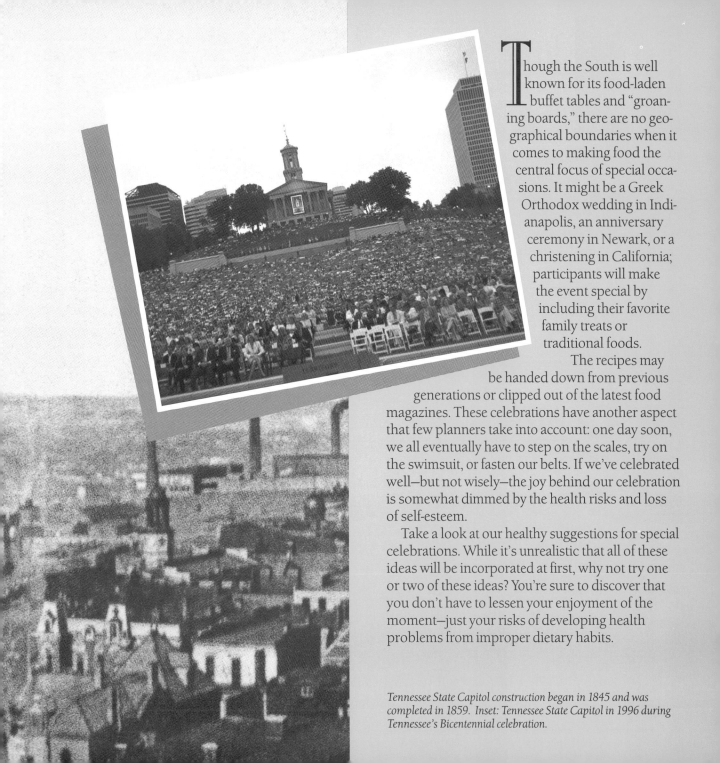

Though the South is well known for its food-laden buffet tables and "groaning boards," there are no geographical boundaries when it comes to making food the central focus of special occasions. It might be a Greek Orthodox wedding in Indianapolis, an anniversary ceremony in Newark, or a christening in California; participants will make the event special by including their favorite family treats or traditional foods.

The recipes may be handed down from previous generations or clipped out of the latest food magazines. These celebrations have another aspect that few planners take into account: one day soon, we all eventually have to step on the scales, try on the swimsuit, or fasten our belts. If we've celebrated well—but not wisely—the joy behind our celebration is somewhat dimmed by the health risks and loss of self-esteem.

Take a look at our healthy suggestions for special celebrations. While it's unrealistic that all of these ideas will be incorporated at first, why not try one or two of these ideas? You're sure to discover that you don't have to lessen your enjoyment of the moment—just your risks of developing health problems from improper dietary habits.

Tennessee State Capitol construction began in 1845 and was completed in 1859. Inset: Tennessee State Capitol in 1996 during Tennessee's Bicentennial celebration.

Then

CHRISTMAS DINNER

Eggnog ♦ Mulled Spiced Cider ♦ Sausage Cheese Balls
Cranberry Salad ♦ Roasted Turkey
Turkey Gravy ♦ Corn Bread Dressing
Candied Sweet Potatoes ♦ Asparagus with Cheese Sauce
Dinner Rolls ♦ Coconut Cake ♦ Fruitcake

CALORIES: 2373; TOTAL FAT: 130 g; CHOLESTEROL: 337 mg; SODIUM: 3587 mg;
CALORIES FROM FAT: 50%

Now

CHRISTMAS DINNER

Marshmallow Creme Eggnog *page 35* ♦ Citrus Punch *page 36* ♦ Holiday Appetizer
Pie *page 36* ♦ Oven-Roasted Turkey *page 18* ♦ Turkey Gravy *page 18* ♦ Chestnut Corn
Bread Dressing *page 19* ♦ Candied Sweet Potatoes *page 37* ♦ Asparagus
Vinaigrette *page 38* ♦ Cranberry Relish *page 38* ♦ Herbed Dinner Rolls *page 39*
Fat-Free Mocha Cake *page 40* ♦ Fireside Coffee *page 41* ♦ Friendship Tea *page 41*

CALORIES: 1127; TOTAL FAT: 11.3 g; CHOLESTEROL: 66 mg; SODIUM: 1030 mg;
CALORIES FROM FAT: 9%

Marshmallow Creme Eggnog

4 cups skim milk
½ cup marshmallow creme
3 tablespoons sugar
1 (4-inch) piece of vanilla bean, split lengthwise
1⅔ cups frozen egg substitute, thawed
½ cup bourbon (optional)
½ teaspoon freshly grated nutmeg (optional)
2 cups vanilla ice milk, softened
Freshly ground nutmeg (optional)

Combine the skim milk, marshmallow creme, sugar and vanilla bean in a saucepan and mix well. Cook over medium-low heat until the marshmallow creme melts, stirring frequently. Stir ¼ of the hot mixture gradually into the egg substitute. Add the egg substitute to the hot mixture, stirring constantly. Cook over low heat for 1 to 2 minutes or until thickened, stirring constantly. Remove from heat. Stir in the bourbon and ½ teaspoon nutmeg. Let stand until cool. Chill, covered, for 3 hours. Discard the vanilla bean. Stir in the ice milk just before serving. Sprinkle each serving with freshly ground nutmeg if desired. **Yield:** 16 (½-cup) servings.

Per Serving:
Calories: 113; Carbohydrate: 13 g; Protein: 5 g; Total Fat: 1 g;
Cholesterol: 4 mg; Sodium: 84 mg; Fiber: trace;
Calories from Fat: 7%

Celebrations

Citrus Punch

¼ cup sugar ♦ ¼ cup water
10 whole cloves ♦ 3 cinnamon sticks
1 quart orange juice
2 cups apple juice ♦ 4 or 5 orange slices

Combine the sugar, water, cloves and cinnamon sticks in a saucepan. Simmer for 10 minutes or until of a syrupy consistency, stirring frequently. Stir in the orange juice and apple juice. Cook just until heated through, stirring occasionally. Pour into a heated tureen. Float the orange slices on top. Ladle into mugs. **Yield:** 10 servings.

Per Serving:
Calories: 87; Carbohydrate: 21 g; Protein: 1 g; Total Fat: trace;
Cholesterol: 0 mg; Sodium: 2 mg; Fiber: trace;
Calories from Fat: 0%

Holiday Appetizer Pie

8 ounces nonfat cream cheese, softened
2 tablespoons skim milk
1 (2½-ounce) jar dried beef, finely chopped
3 tablespoons minced dried onion
2 tablespoons finely chopped green bell pepper
⅛ teaspoon pepper ♦ ½ cup nonfat sour cream
¼ cup coarsely chopped English walnuts

Beat the cream cheese and skim milk in a bowl until blended. Stir in the dried beef, onion, green pepper and pepper. Add the sour cream and mix well. Spoon into an 8-inch pie plate or shallow baking dish. Sprinkle with the walnuts. Bake at 350 degrees for 15 minutes. Yield: 24 (2-tablespoon) servings.

Per Serving:
Calories: 29; Carbohydrate: 2.6 g; Protein: 2.6 g; Total Fat: 0.9 g;
Cholesterol: trace; Sodium: 159 mg; Fiber: trace;
Calories from Fat: 28%

CANDIED SWEET POTATOES

2½ pounds sweet potatoes
⅓ cup packed brown sugar
2 tablespoons reduced-calorie margarine
2 tablespoons unsweetened orange juice

Place the sweet potatoes in a heavy saucepan. Add just enough water to cover. Bring to a boil; reduce heat. Simmer, covered, for 20 minutes or until the sweet potatoes are tender; drain. Let stand until cool. Peel the sweet potatoes and cut into 1½-inch pieces. Place in a large bowl. Combine the brown sugar, margarine and orange juice in a saucepan. Cook over medium heat until the margarine melts, stirring constantly. Pour over the sweet potatoes, tossing gently to coat. Serve immediately. Yield: 6 servings.

PER SERVING:
CALORIES: 207; CARBOHYDRATE: 45 g; PROTEIN: 2.4 g; TOTAL FAT: 2.5 g;
CHOLESTEROL: 0 mg; SODIUM: 37.5 mg; FIBER: trace;
CALORIES FROM FAT: 11%

A recommended margarine should have "liquid oil" as the first ingredient and should contain twice the polyunsaturated–versus saturated–fats.

CELEBRATIONS

ASPARAGUS VINAIGRETTE

3¾ pounds asparagus spears ♦ ½ cup rice vinegar ♦ ¼ cup water
¼ cup lemon juice ♦ 1 (4-ounce) jar diced pimentos, drained
2 teaspoons olive oil ♦ 1 teaspoon dry mustard
1 teaspoon grated lemon peel ♦ 1 teaspoon white pepper

Snap off the tough ends of the asparagus. Remove the scales. Combine the asparagus with just enough water to cover in a saucepan. Bring to a boil. Cook for 6 to 8 minutes or until tender-crisp; drain. Arrange the asparagus in a 9x13-inch dish. Pour a mixture of the remaining ingredients over the asparagus. Chill. Remove the asparagus to a serving platter using a slotted spoon. **Yield:** 16 servings.

Per Serving:
Calories: 24; Carbohydrate: 3.3 g; Protein: 2.3 g; Total Fat: 0.7 g;
Cholesterol: 0 mg; Sodium: 3 mg; Fiber: trace;
Calories from Fat: 27%
Nutritional profile includes entire amount of vinaigrette.

CRANBERRY RELISH

1 orange, cut into quarters, seeded ♦ 2 cups fresh cranberries
1 cup chopped Red Delicious apple
1 (8-ounce) can unsweetened crushed pineapple, drained
⅓ cup sugar ♦ Fresh spinach leaves (optional)

Process the orange in a food processor until chopped. Process the cranberries in the food processor until coarsely ground. Combine the cranberries, apple, pineapple and sugar with the orange in a bowl. Chill, covered, for 8 hours . Line individual serving plates with spinach. Spoon ¼ cup of the relish onto each plate. **Yield:** 12 (¼-cup) servings.

Per Serving:
Calories: 52; Carbohydrate: 13.5 g; Protein: 0.3 g; Total Fat: 0.1 g;
Cholesterol: 0 mg; Sodium: 0 mg; Fiber: trace;
Calories from Fat: 2%

Herbed Dinner Rolls

2 envelopes dry yeast ♦ ½ cup warm (105- to 115-degree) water
1 cup skim milk
2 tablespoons margarine ♦ 1 tablespoon sugar
1 teaspoon Italian seasoning
½ teaspoon salt ♦ ¼ teaspoon garlic powder
¼ cup frozen egg substitute, thawed ♦ 2 cups whole wheat flour
¼ cup grated fat-free Parmesan cheese
2½ cups (about) all-purpose flour ♦ 2 tablespoons all-purpose flour

Dissolve the yeast in the warm water in a mixer bowl and mix well. Combine the skim milk, margarine, sugar, Italian seasoning, salt and garlic powder in a saucepan. Cook over medium heat until the margarine melts, stirring occasionally. Cool to 105 to 115 degrees. Add the milk mixture, egg substitute and whole wheat flour to the yeast mixture. Beat at low speed just until blended. Beat at high speed for 3 minutes longer, scraping the bowl occasionally. Add the cheese and just enough of the 2½ cups all-purpose flour to make a stiff dough and mix well. Sprinkle 1 tablespoon of the all-purpose flour evenly over the work surface. Turn the dough onto the floured surface. Knead for 5 to 7 minutes or until smooth and elastic. Place the dough in a bowl sprayed with nonstick cooking spray, turning to coat the surface. Let rise, covered, in a warm place (85 degrees) free from drafts for 45 minutes or until doubled in bulk. Punch the dough down. Sprinkle the remaining 1 tablespoon all-purpose flour onto the work surface. Turn the dough onto the work surface. Let rest, covered, for 10 minutes. Shape the dough into 30 balls. Arrange 15 balls in each of two 9-inch round baking pans sprayed with nonstick cooking spray. Let rise, covered, in a warm place free from drafts for 35 minutes or until doubled in bulk. Bake at 375 degrees for 25 minutes or until golden brown. Remove from the pans. Serve warm.
Yield: 30 (1-roll) servings.

Per Serving:
Calories: 81; Carbohydrate: 1 g; Protein: 3 g; Total Fat: 1 g;
Cholesterol: 1 mg; Sodium: 69 mg; Fiber: 1 g;
Calories from Fat: 14%

Celebrations

Fat-Free Mocha Cake

Cake
1⅓ cups packed brown sugar
1 cup flour
⅓ cup plus 1 tablespoon baking cocoa
1 teaspoon instant coffee or espresso powder
1 teaspoon baking powder
1 teaspoon baking soda
6 egg whites
1 cup coffee low-fat yogurt
1 teaspoon vanilla extract
Raspberry Amaretto Sauce
2 cups fresh or thawed frozen raspberries
½ cup confectioners' sugar
¼ cup amaretto
1 tablespoon fresh lemon juice

For the cake, combine the brown sugar, flour, baking cocoa, coffee, baking powder and baking soda in a bowl and mix well. Mix the egg whites, yogurt and vanilla in a bowl. Fold the brown sugar mixture into the egg white mixture. Spoon into a 9-inch round or square cake pan sprayed with nonstick cooking spray. Bake at 350 degrees for 30 minutes.

For the sauce, process the raspberries, confectioners' sugar, amaretto and lemon juice in a blender or food processor until puréed; strain the sauce.

Cut the cake into 18 slices. Spoon 4 teaspoons of the sauce over each serving. **Yield:** 18 servings.

Per Serving:
Calories: 119; Carbohydrate: 25 g; Protein: 3 g; Total Fat: 1 g;
Cholesterol: 1 mg; Sodium: 105 mg; Fiber: 1 g;
Calories from Fat: trace

FIRESIDE COFFEE MIX

2 cups fat-free coffee creamer
1½ cups hot cocoa mix
1½ cups instant coffee granules
1½ cups sugar ♦ 1 teaspoon cinnamon
½ teaspoon nutmeg

Combine the creamer, cocoa mix, coffee granules, sugar, cinnamon and nutmeg in a bowl and mix well. Store in an airtight container. Combine 3 tablespoons of the coffee mix with 1 cup boiling water in a mug for each serving. **Yield:** 35 (3-tablespoon) servings.

PER SERVING:
CALORIES: 89; CARBOHYDRATE: 20 g; PROTEIN: trace; TOTAL FAT: trace;
CHOLESTEROL: trace; SODIUM: 24 mg; FIBER: trace;
CALORIES FROM FAT: 2.5%

FRIENDSHIP TEA MIX

1 (18-ounce) jar orange instant breakfast drink mix
1 cup sugar
½ cup sweetened lemonade mix
½ cup instant tea ♦ 1 (3-ounce) package apricot gelatin
2½ teaspoons cinnamon
1 teaspoon ground cloves

Combine the breakfast drink mix, sugar, lemonade mix, instant tea, gelatin, cinnamon and cloves in a bowl and mix well. To serve, spoon 1½ tablespoons of the mix into a cup. Add 1 cup boiling water and mix well. Store the mix in an airtight container.
Yield: 50 servings.

PER SERVING:
CALORIES: 94; CARBOHYDRATE: 45 g; PROTEIN: 0.2 g; TOTAL FAT: 0 g;
CHOLESTEROL: 0 mg; SODIUM: 33 mg; FIBER: trace;
CALORIES FROM FAT: 0%

Easter Dinner

Ambrosia *page 42*
Honey-Glazed Ham Slices *page 43*
Mashed Potatoes *page 20*
Gingered Carrots *page 43*
Country Green Beans *page 20*
Yogurt Dinner Rolls *page 21*
Easter Basket Trifle *page 44*
Iced Fruit Tea

Ambrosia

Sections of 3 medium pink grapefruit
Sections of 3 large oranges
1 medium Red Delicious apple, sliced
½ cup unsweetened orange juice ♦ ¼ teaspoon coconut extract
Fresh mint sprigs (optional)

Combine the grapefruit sections, orange sections, apple, orange juice and flavoring in a bowl and mix gently. Chill, covered, for 1 hour or longer. Spoon into lettuce cups. Top with mint sprigs. **Yield:** 12 servings.

PER SERVING:
CALORIES: 50; CARBOHYDRATE: 12.6 g; PROTEIN: 0.8 g; TOTAL FAT: 0.2 g;
CHOLESTEROL: 0 mg; SODIUM: 0 mg; FIBER: 2.7 g;
CALORIES FROM FAT: 4%

Honey-Glazed Ham Slices

6 (3-ounce) slices lean lower-salt cooked ham, ¼ inch thick
6 juice-pack canned pineapple slices
½ cup packed brown sugar
½ cup honey
½ teaspoon dry mustard

Arrange the ham slices in a 9x13-inch baking dish sprayed with nonstick cooking spray. Place 1 pineapple slice on each ham slice. Combine the brown sugar, honey and dry mustard in a saucepan and mix well. Bring to a boil over medium heat. Boil for 2 minutes, stirring occasionally. Spoon over the pineapple slices. Bake at 325 degrees for 15 minutes or until heated through. **Yield:** 6 servings.

Per Serving:
Calories: 242; Carbohydrate: 37 g; Protein: 15 g; Total Fat: 4 g;
Cholesterol: 42 mg; Sodium: 860 mg; Fiber: trace;
Calories from Fat: 16%

Gingered Carrots

1 pound carrots, peeled, cut into ¼-inch slices
1 tablespoon reduced-calorie margarine
1 tablespoon sugar ♦ 1 teaspoon grated fresh gingerroot
2 tablespoons finely chopped fresh parsley

Steam the carrots in a steamer for 15 to 20 minutes or until tender-crisp. Remove from heat. Heat the margarine in a skillet over medium heat until it bubbles. Add the carrots, tossing to coat. Sprinkle with the sugar and gingerroot, tossing to coat. Cook for 1 to 2 minutes or until the carrots are lightly glazed. Sprinkle with the parsley. Serve immediately. **Yield:** 5 servings.

Per Serving:
Calories: 65; Carbohydrate: 11 g; Protein: 1 g; Total Fat: 2 g;
Cholesterol: 0 mg; Sodium: 76 mg; Fiber: trace;
Calories from Fat: 27%

"Select" grades of meat are lower in fat than "choice." "Choice" grades are lower in fat than "prime."

Celebrations

Try angel food cake, fig bars, and gingersnaps as substitutes for commercial baked goods high in saturated fat.

Easter Basket Trifle

1 (10½-ounce) loaf angel food cake
1½ cups skim milk
½ cup 1% cottage cheese ♦ ¼ cup sugar
3 tablespoons cornstarch
2 tablespoons instant nonfat dry milk powder
1 tablespoon grated orange peel
2 teaspoons vanilla extract
½ cup reduced-calorie strawberry spread
5 cups fresh strawberry halves
5 kiwifruit, thinly sliced ♦ Sections of 4 medium oranges
Fresh blueberries (optional)
Fresh red raspberries (optional)

Cut the angel food cake into 1-inch cubes. Combine the skim milk, cottage cheese, sugar, cornstarch and milk powder in a blender or food processor container. Process until smooth. Pour into a double boiler. Bring the water to a boil; reduce heat to medium-low. Cook for 10 to 12 minutes or until thickened, stirring constantly. Remove from heat. Stir in the orange peel and vanilla. Spoon into a bowl. Chill, covered, in the refrigerator. Bring the strawberry spread to a boil in a saucepan, stirring constantly. Remove from heat. Arrange ½ of the angel food cake cubes in a 3-quart trifle bowl. Brush with half of the strawberry spread. Arrange enough of the strawberry halves cut side out to line the lower edge of the bowl. Place half the remaining strawberries over the angel food cake cubes. Top with ½ of the kiwifruit and ½ of the orange sections. Spread with ½ of the chilled custard. Repeat the procedure with the remaining angel food cake cubes, strawberry spread, fruit and custard. Chill, covered, for 8 hours. Top with blueberries and raspberries just before serving.
Yield: 12 servings.

Per Serving:
Calories: 171; Carbohydrate: 38 g; Protein: 5 g; Total Fat: 1 g;
Cholesterol: 1 mg; Sodium: 99 mg; Fiber: 4 g;
Calories from Fat: 4%

Backyard Barbecue

Fresh Vegetables with Easy Nonfat Yogurt Dip *page 45*
Fresh Fruit with Fruit Dip *page 46*
Potato Salad *page 46*
Barbecued Shrimp *page 47* or
Grilled Chicken with Tangy Barbecue Sauce
Heart-Healthy Baked Beans *page 48*
Grilled Corn on the Cob
Totally Free Deviled Eggs *page 49*
French Bread
Strawberry Ice Cream *page 49*

Easy Nonfat Yogurt Dip

½ cup plain nonfat yogurt
½ cup nonfat ranch salad dressing
½ teaspoon dillweed ♦ ¼ teaspoon pepper

Combine the yogurt, salad dressing, dillweed and pepper in a bowl and mix well. Serve with fresh vegetables of your choice. May substitute your favorite nonfat salad dressing for the ranch salad dressing. **Yield:** 8 (2-tablespoon) servings.

Per Serving:
Calories: 30.4; Carbohydrate: 5.6 g; Protein: 1.3 g; Total Fat: 0 g;
Cholesterol: trace; Sodium: 170 mg; Fiber: trace;
Calories from Fat: 0%

Fruit Dip

1 (7½-ounce) jar marshmallow creme
8 ounces nonfat cream cheese, softened
2 tablespoons apricot preserves

Beat the marshmallow creme, cream cheese and apricot preserves in a mixer bowl until blended. Chill, covered, until serving time. Serve with fresh fruit chunks. **Yield:** 16 (2-tablespoon) servings.

Per Serving:
Calories: 61; Carbohydrate: 13.4 g; Protein: 2.1 g; Total Fat: 0 g;
Cholesterol: 1.5 mg; Sodium: 76 mg; Fiber: trace;
Calories from Fat: 0%

Potato Salad

1¼ pounds unpeeled potatoes ♦ ¾ cup sliced celery
½ cup chopped green bell pepper ♦ ⅓ cup finely chopped onion
¼ cup grated carrot ♦ 2 tablespoons sweet pickle relish
½ cup fat-free mayonnaise ♦ ½ cup nonfat sour cream
1 teaspoon mustard with horseradish
1 teaspoon prepared mustard ♦ ¼ teaspoon salt
¼ teaspoon celery seeds ♦ 1 clove of garlic, minced
2 hard-cooked egg whites, chopped

Combine the potatoes with enough water to cover in a saucepan. Bring to a boil. Cook, covered, for 25 to 30 minutes or until tender; drain and cool. Peel and coarsely chop the potatoes. Transfer to a large bowl. Stir in the celery, green pepper, onion, carrot and pickle relish. Mix the next 7 ingredients in a bowl. Add to the potatoes, tossing gently to coat. Fold in the egg whites. Chill, covered, for 4 to 24 hours. Serve in a lettuce-lined bowl. **Yield:** 8 servings.

Per Serving:
Calories: 85; Carbohydrate: 18.7 g; Protein: 2.4 g; Total Fat: 0.2 g;
Cholesterol: 1.5 mg; Sodium: 278 mg; Fiber: trace;
Calories from Fat: 2%

Barbecued Shrimp

½ onion, finely chopped
2 teaspoons olive oil or vegetable oil
1 (6-ounce) can no-salt-added tomato sauce
2 tablespoons vinegar
2 tablespoons brown sugar
2 tablespoons dry mustard
2 teaspoons oregano
½ teaspoon garlic powder
5 drops of Tabasco sauce
24 large shrimp, peeled, deveined
Lemon or lime wedges

Sauté the onion in the olive oil in a small saucepan until tender. Stir in the tomato sauce, vinegar, brown sugar, dry mustard, oregano, garlic powder and Tabasco sauce. Cook over low heat for 5 minutes, stirring occasionally. Remove from heat. Let stand until cool. Pour over the shrimp in a bowl, turning to coat. Chill, covered, for 4 to 10 hours, turning occasionally. Thread the shrimp on skewers. Arrange the skewers on a broiler pan. Broil close to heat source for 3 to 4 minutes per side or until the shrimp turn pink. Serve with lemon or lime wedges. **Yield:** 6 servings.

Per Serving:
Calories: 71; Carbohydrate: 7.1 g; Protein: 6.3 g; Total Fat: 2 g;
Cholesterol: 43 mg; Sodium: 50 mg; Fiber: trace;
Calories from Fat: 25%

Heart-Healthy Baked Beans

3 cups dried navy beans
4 quarts water
1 onion, finely chopped
1 clove of garlic
¼ teaspoon salt
1 cup packed brown sugar
½ cup chili sauce
1 tablespoon Worcestershire sauce
1 teaspoon dry mustard

Sort and rinse the navy beans. Combine the beans with 2 quarts of the water in a bowl. Let stand for 8 to 10 hours; drain. (Or cover the beans with 2 quarts of water and bring to a boil in a saucepan. Remove from heat. Let stand, covered, for 1 hour; drain.) Combine the beans, onion, garlic and salt with the remaining 2 quarts water in a heavy saucepan. Bring to a boil; reduce heat. Simmer for 1½ to 2 hours or until the beans are tender. Add hot water as needed to keep the beans covered while cooking. (Or, use a pressure cooker. Combine the beans with the onion, garlic and salt and just enough water to cover. Close the pressure cooker. Steam for 3 to 5 minutes or until the steam smells like cooked beans. Remove from heat; cool the side with cold water.) Drain the excess water. Stir in the brown sugar, chili sauce, Worcestershire sauce and dry mustard. Spoon into a bean pot or baking dish. Bake, covered, at 300 degrees for 1 hour. **Yield:** 8 servings.

Per Serving:
Calories: 267; Carbohydrate: 55 g; Protein: 11 g; Total Fat: 0.6 g;
Cholesterol: 0 mg; Sodium: 299 mg; Fiber: 4.45 g;
Calories from Fat: 2%

TOTALLY FREE DEVILED EGGS

½ cup egg substitute ♦ ½ cup nonfat mayonnaise
2 tablespoons pickle relish, drained
1 tablespoon prepared mustard ♦ ¼ teaspoon pepper
10 hard-cooked eggs ♦ Paprika to taste

Pour the egg substitute into an 8-inch skillet sprayed with nonstick cooking spray. Cook, covered, over low heat for 5 minutes or just until set. Let stand until cool. Chop and mash the egg substitute. Combine the egg substitute with the mayonnaise, pickle relish, prepared mustard and pepper in a bowl and mix well. Slice the hard-cooked eggs into halves; discard the yolks. Spoon approximately 1 tablespoon of the egg substitute mixture into each egg white half. Chill, covered, until serving time. Sprinkle with paprika. Process the mayonnaise, pickle relish, prepared mustard and pepper in a blender for a fluffy texture. **Yield:** 20 servings.

PER SERVING:
CALORIES: 17.5; CARBOHYDRATE: 1.4 g; PROTEIN: 2 g; TOTAL FAT: 0 g;
CHOLESTEROL: 0 mg; SODIUM: 95 mg; FIBER: trace;
CALORIES FROM FAT: 0%

STRAWBERRY ICE CREAM

2 egg whites ♦ 1 cup sugar
⅛ teaspoon salt ♦ 1 pint fresh strawberries, chopped

Combine the egg whites, sugar and salt in a mixer bowl. Beat at high speed for 5 minutes, scraping the bowl occasionally; do not cut time. Add the strawberries. Beat at high speed for 15 minutes, scraping the bowl occasionally. Spoon into a freezer container. Freeze, covered, until firm. **Yield:** 4 servings.

PER SERVING:
CALORIES: 223; CARBOHYDRATE: 55 g; PROTEIN: 2 g; TOTAL FAT: trace;
CHOLESTEROL: 0 mg; SODIUM: 98 mg; FIBER: 1 g;
CALORIES FROM FAT: trace

Meats lower in fat
are also generally less
tender. Marinating these
for a few hours
will enhance flavor and
increase tenderness.

COMPANY DINNER

Herbed Pot Roast *page 50* ◆ Country Green Beans *page 20*
Baked Apples *page 51* ◆ Yogurt Dinner Rolls *page 21*
Sweet Potato Pie *page 51*

HERBED POT ROAST

1 (4½-pound) lean boneless rump roast, trimmed
½ cup burgundy or other dry red wine
½ cup no-salt-added tomato sauce
¼ cup vinegar ◆ 1 tablespoon spicy hot mustard
1 teaspoon whole thyme ◆ ¼ teaspoon whole oregano
¼ teaspoon ground red pepper ◆ 2 shallots, minced
1 bay leaf ◆ 1 pound carrots, peeled, cut into quarters
12 new potatoes, cut into quarters ◆ 6 small onions, cut into halves

Place the roast in a sealable plastic bag. Pour a mixture of the next 8 ingredients over the roast. Add the bay leaf; seal tightly. Marinate in the refrigerator for up to 8 hours. Transfer the roast and marinade to a large roasting pan. Add the carrots, potatoes and onions. Bake, covered, for 2½ hours or until the roast is of the desired doneness. Place the roast on a serving platter. Let stand for 10 minutes before slicing. Arrange the carrots, potatoes and onions around the roast; discard the marinade and bay leaf. **Yield:** 15 (3 ounces roast with vegetables) servings.

PER SERVING:
CALORIES: 248; CARBOHYDRATE: 15 g; PROTEIN: 32.8 g; TOTAL FAT: 5.6 g;
CHOLESTEROL: 78 mg; SODIUM: 98 mg; FIBER: trace;
CALORIES FROM FAT: 20%
Nutritional profile includes entire amount of marinade.

Baked Apples

8 unpeeled cooking apples, cut into bite-size pieces
½ cup packed brown sugar ♦ ¼ cup chopped walnuts
1 teaspoon cinnamon

Combine the apples, brown sugar, walnuts and cinnamon in a bowl and mix gently. Spoon into a baking dish. Bake, covered, at 350 degrees for 1 hour, removing the cover after 30 to 45 minutes if the apples appear to be too juicy. **Yield:** 8 servings.

Per Serving:
Calories: 138; Carbohydrate: 31 g; Protein: 8 g; Total Fat: 3 g;
Cholesterol: 0 mg; Sodium: 4 mg; Fiber: 3 g;
Calories from Fat: 19%

Sweet Potato Pie

2 cups mashed cooked sweet potatoes
1 cup egg substitute ♦ 1 cup packed brown sugar
1 teaspoon vanilla extract ♦ ½ teaspoon ginger
½ teaspoon cinnamon ♦ ½ teaspoon nutmeg
⅛ teaspoon ground cloves
1¾ cups evaporated skim milk
1 unbaked (9-inch) Low-Fat Pie Crust (page 138)

Blend the sweet potatoes, egg substitute, brown sugar, vanilla, ginger, cinnamon, nutmeg and cloves in a mixer bowl at medium speed. Stir in the evaporated milk. Spoon into the pie shell. Bake at 450 degrees for 15 minutes; reduce the oven temperature to 300 degrees. Bake for 30 minutes longer or until set. Cool. **Yield:** 8 servings.

Per Serving:
Calories: 246; Carbohydrate: 54 g; Protein: 7.3 g; Total Fat: trace;
Cholesterol: 1.7 mg; Sodium: 131 mg; Fiber: trace;
Calories from Fat: 0%
Nutritional profile does not include the pie shell.

Some things in life cannot be changed. Accept this.

CELEBRATIONS

Special Luncheon

Sliced Basil Tomatoes or Chilled Strawberry Soup *page 52*
Chicken Salad with Poppy Seed Dressing *page 53*
Steamed Asparagus Spears
Mandarin Orange Sections or
Honeydew and Cantaloupe Cubes
Banana Yogurt Bread *page 54* or Crusty French Bread
Frozen Sorbet ◆ Iced Tea or Spiced Iced Tea *page 54*

Chilled Strawberry Soup

2 pints fresh or frozen strawberries ◆ ½ cup dry Champagne
¼ cup skim milk ◆ ½ cup plain nonfat yogurt
2 tablespoons honey

Process the strawberries in a blender or food processor until puréed. Add the Champagne, skim milk, yogurt and honey. Process until blended. Chill until serving time. Ladle into soup bowls. Garnish with light whipped topping, fresh strawberries and/or fresh mint sprigs. May substitute a mixture of ¼ cup sparkling water and ¼ cup white grape juice for the Champagne. Sprinkle the strawberries with ¼ cup sugar and chill for 8 to 10 hours before processing to yield a sweeter soup; omit the honey. **Yield:** 6 (½-cup) servings.

Per Serving:
Calories: 90; Carbohydrate: 15 g; Protein: 2 g; Total Fat: 0.5 g;
Cholesterol: 5 mg; Sodium: 23 mg; Fiber: trace;
Calories from Fat: 5%

Chicken Salad with Poppy Seed Dressing

4 boneless skinless chicken breasts
1 cup red seedless grape halves ♦ ½ cup chopped celery
2 tablespoons slivered almonds, toasted
½ cup commercial fat-free poppy seed salad dressing

Rinse the chicken. Combine the chicken with enough water to cover in a saucepan. Cook until tender; drain. Chill, covered, in the refrigerator. Cut the chicken into bite-size pieces. Combine the chicken, grapes, celery and almonds in a bowl. Add the salad dressing, tossing to coat. Spoon onto lettuce-lined plates.
Yield: 4 (1-cup salad and 2-tablespoons dressing) servings.

PER SERVING:
CALORIES: 278; CARBOHYDRATE: 23.5 g; PROTEIN: 29 g; TOTAL FAT: 6.6 g;
CHOLESTEROL: 73 mg; SODIUM: 248 mg; FIBER: trace;
CALORIES FROM FAT: 21%

Poppy Seed Dressing

1 tablespoon cornstarch ♦ 1 teaspoon sugar
½ teaspoon dry mustard ♦ 1 cup water
3 tablespoons honey
2 tablespoons vinegar ♦ 2 teaspoons poppy seeds

Combine the cornstarch, sugar and dry mustard in a saucepan and mix well. Stir in the water, honey and vinegar. Bring to a boil; reduce heat. Cook until thickened, stirring constantly. Cool slightly. Stir in the poppy seeds. Chill, covered, until serving time.
Yield: 20 (1-tablespoon) servings.

PER SERVING:
CALORIES: 12; CARBOHYDRATE: 6 g; PROTEIN: 0 g; TOTAL FAT: 0.1 g;
CHOLESTEROL: 0 mg; SODIUM: 0 mg; FIBER: 0 g;
CALORIES FROM FAT: 8%

Beware of the "No Cholesterol" tag. This simply means that a product does not contain animal fat. It may still contain a large amount of total fat, particularly saturated fats.

CELEBRATIONS

53

Banana Yogurt Bread

2 teaspoons flour ♦ 2 cups flour ♦ 1½ teaspoons baking powder
½ teaspoon baking soda ♦ ¼ teaspoon salt
1 cup plain nonfat yogurt ♦ 1 cup mashed ripe banana
½ cup sugar ♦ ¼ cup canola oil ♦ 2 egg whites, lightly beaten
1 egg, lightly beaten ♦ 1 teaspoon vanilla extract

Spray a 5x9-inch loaf pan with nonstick cooking spray; sprinkle with 2 teaspoons flour. Mix 2 cups flour, baking powder, baking soda and salt in a bowl. Make a well in the center of the dry ingredients. Add a mixture of the yogurt, banana, sugar, canola oil, egg whites, egg and vanilla to the well, mixing just until moistened. Spoon into the prepared loaf pan. Bake at 350 degrees for 1 hour or until the loaf tests done. Cool in the pan for 10 minutes. Invert onto a wire rack to cool completely. **Yield:** 18 (½-inch slice) servings.

Per Serving:
Calories: 123; Carbohydrate: 21 g; Protein: 3 g; Total Fat: 3 g;
Cholesterol: 13 mg; Sodium: 130 mg; Fiber: trace;
Calories from Fat: 22%

Spiced Iced Tea

16 cups water ♦ 1 teaspoon cardamom seeds
1 teaspoon whole allspice ♦ 3 (3-inch) cinnamon sticks, halved
8 tea bags ♦ Fresh mint sprigs (optional)

Combine the water, cardamom seeds, allspice and cinnamon sticks in a large heavy saucepan. Bring to a boil. Remove from heat. Add the tea bags. Steep, covered, for 5 minutes. Strain the tea into a heatproof pitcher. Chill until serving time. Serve in glasses over ice. Top each glass with a mint sprig. **Yield:** 16 (1 cup) servings.

Per Serving:
Calories: 2; Carbohydrate: 0.6 g; Protein: 0.1 g; Total Fat: 0 g;
Cholesterol: 0 mg; Sodium: 0 mg; Fiber: trace;
Calories from Fat: 0%

Outdoor Feast

Fruit Salad *page 55*
Chicken Kabobs *page 56*
Grilled Potatoes and Vegetables *page 57*
Marinated Vegetables *page 57*
French Bread

Fruit Salad

1 (15-ounce) can juice-pack sliced peaches
1 (15-ounce) can juice-pack apricots
1 (15-ounce) can juice-pack pineapple
1 (15-ounce) can mandarin oranges
2 small packages fat-free vanilla instant pudding mix
2 tablespoons orange instant breakfast drink mix
2 tablespoons lemon juice ♦ 3 cups green grapes
1 pint fresh strawberries, cut into halves ♦ 4 bananas, sliced

Drain the peaches, apricots, pineapple and mandarin oranges, reserving the juice. Combine the reserved juice, pudding mix, drink mix and lemon juice in a bowl and mix well. Stir in the peaches, apricots, pineapple and mandarin oranges. Add the grapes, strawberries and bananas, stirring gently. Chill, covered, for several hours before serving. **Yield:** 22 (¾-cup) servings.

Per Serving:
Calories: 117; Carbohydrate: 31.3 g; Protein: 0.8 g; Total Fat: trace;
Cholesterol: 0 mg; Sodium: 132 mg; Fiber: trace;
Calories from Fat: 2%

CHICKEN KABOBS

4 chicken breasts halves, skinned, boned
½ cup fat-free Italian salad dressing
⅓ cup liquid smoke
1 tablespoon brown sugar
¼ teaspoon pepper
⅛ teaspoon garlic powder
2 medium onions, cut into 4 wedges
8 cherry tomatoes
1 green bell pepper, cut into wedges
8 mushrooms

Rinse the chicken and pat dry. Cut into 1-inch pieces. Place in a shallow dish. Combine the salad dressing, liquid smoke, brown sugar, pepper and garlic powder in a bowl and mix well. Pour over the chicken, tossing to coat. Marinate, covered, in the refrigerator for several hours, turning occasionally; drain. Thread the chicken, onions, cherry tomatoes, green pepper and mushrooms alternately onto skewers. Grill 4 to 5 inches above hot coals for 8 to 10 minutes or until the chicken is cooked through, turning after 4 minutes. Serve with hot cooked long grain and wild rice. **Yield:** 4 servings.

PER SERVING:
CALORIES: 222; CARBOHYDRATE: 13 g; PROTEIN: 27 g; TOTAL FAT: 3.5 g;
CHOLESTEROL: 73 mg; SODIUM: 631 mg; FIBER: trace;
CALORIES FROM FAT: 14%
Nutritional profile includes entire amount of marinade.

Grilled Potatoes and Vegetables

4 potatoes, cut into 2-inch wedges ♦ 1 large onion, cut into wedges
1 zucchini, cut into chunks
2 yellow summer squash, cut into chunks ♦ 1 teaspoon basil
1 teaspoon thyme ♦ 1 teaspoon paprika ♦ 1 teaspoon garlic powder

Combine the potatoes with enough water to cover in a microwave-safe bowl. Microwave on High until tender-crisp; drain. Thread the potatoes, onion, zucchini and summer squash on skewers. Spray with butter-flavor nonstick cooking spray. Sprinkle with a mixture of the seasonings. Grill over hot coals until brown and of the desired degree of doneness, turning occasionally. **Yield:** 4 servings.

Per Serving:
Calories: 117; Carbohydrate: 26 g; Protein: 3 g; Total Fat: 0.4 g;
Cholesterol: 0 mg; Sodium: 10 mg; Fiber: trace;
Calories from Fat: 3%

Marinated Vegetables

2 pounds carrots, sliced ♦ 2 medium onions, chopped
2 green bell peppers, chopped
1 (10-ounce) can low-sodium tomato soup
¾ cup vinegar ♦ ¾ cup sugar ♦ ¼ cup pineapple juice
3 tablespoons corn oil ♦ 1 teaspoon Worcestershire sauce
1 teaspoon prepared mustard

Cook the carrots in boiling water in a saucepan until tender; drain. Layer the carrots, onions and green peppers in a dish. Pour a mixture of the remaining ingredients over the vegetables. Chill, covered, for 24 hours before serving. **Yield:** 24 servings.

Per Serving:
Calories: 70; Carbohydrate: 13 g; Protein: 0.7 g; Total Fat: 2.0 g;
Cholesterol: 0 mg; Sodium: 21 mg; Fiber: 0.7 g;
Calories from Fat: 26%
Nutritional profile includes entire amount of marinade.

Celebrations

Beat the Clock

W ho hasn't—at one time or another—been responsible for answering the question, "what'll we have for dinner?" It's a daily occurrence for most of us, with fewer and fewer exciting answers. Most people find personal time their least-plentiful commodity, regardless of their age, employment status, or financial resources. We all have to eat, yet we're all busier than ever. And we know that one of the surest ways to wreak havoc with diet and fitness is to visit fast-food "drive-throughs" too frequently.

Perhaps no single solution has helped save time in the kitchen more than the microwave, which is one of our best timesaving devices. It's now also possible to breeze through most local produce departments, picking up "semi-prepared" salads or fresh veggies, allowing us the benefits of fresh vegetables minus the hassle of peeling, slicing, and dicing. Or perhaps a "salad bar to go" is a good ally in your race against time. But remember, being short on time shouldn't mean that you completely abandon good habits, even though it sometimes seems as if preparing healthy food fast is a bigger challenge than you wish to face at the end of the day. What to do? Here are five menu suggestions that'll help solve that nightly time crunch. Whether you're racing home to prepare a weeknight dinner for the boss (see Chicken Marsala), spending a quiet night with your significant other, or just making a commitment to spend less time in the kitchen, here are some ideas for meals that will get you in and out of the food prep area and still allow time for a nice walk before dark.

Nashville's Second Avenue in 1896 during Tennessee's Centennial celebration. Inset: Second Avenue in 1996.

CHICKEN MARSALA THEN

4 whole chicken breasts, split, skinned, boned
½ cup melted butter
½ cup chopped green onions
½ teaspoon salt
½ cup marsala
1 cup whipping cream
1 cup fresh mushrooms, sliced
½ cup black olives

PER SERVING:
CALORIES: 376;
CARBOHYDRATE: 2 g;
PROTEIN: 28 g;
TOTAL FAT: 27 g;
CHOLESTEROL: 148 mg;
SODIUM: 287 mg;
FIBER: trace;
CALORIES FROM FAT: 65%

BEAT THE CLOCK

CHICKEN MARSALA NOW

3 whole chicken breasts, split, skinned, boned
¼ cup egg substitute ♦ ¼ cup skim milk
½ cup flour ♦ ¼ teaspoon salt
¼ teaspoon pepper
8 ounces mushrooms, sliced
1 small green bell pepper, cut into strips
½ cup chopped green onions
1 clove of garlic, minced ♦ 1 cup marsala
2 tablespoons brown sugar
1 tablespoon lemon juice
1 low-sodium chicken bouillon cube

Rinse the chicken and pat dry. Pound ¼ inch thick between sheets of waxed paper. Combine the egg substitute and skim milk in a bowl and mix well. Combine the flour, salt and pepper in a bowl and mix well. Dip the chicken into the egg mixture; coat all sides with the flour mixture. Chill for 2 hours. Brown the chicken on both sides in a skillet sprayed with butter-flavor nonstick cooking spray. Cook until the chicken is cooked through. Remove to a platter. Sauté the mushrooms, green pepper, green onions and garlic in the skillet until tender-crisp. Spoon over the chicken. Add the wine, brown sugar, lemon juice and bouillon cube to the skillet. Cook until heated through, stirring frequently. Spoon over the chicken and sautéed vegetables. **Yield:** 6 servings.

PER SERVING:
CALORIES: 237; CARBOHYDRATE: 15 g; PROTEIN: 29 g; TOTAL FAT: 3 g;
CHOLESTEROL: 73 mg; SODIUM: 180 mg; FIBER: trace;
CALORIES FROM FAT: 12%

Menu

Tomato Rice Soup *page 61*
Steak Salad for Two *page 62*
Grilled Garlic Bagels *page 62*
Yogurt Brownies *page 63*

Tomato Rice Soup

⅓ cup chopped celery
⅓ cup chopped onion
1 (28-ounce) can tomatoes, puréed
1 (28-ounce) tomato can water
1 (10¾-ounce) can low-sodium chicken broth
½ teaspoon basil
½ teaspoon curry powder
Pepper to taste
½ cup rice

Sauté the celery and onion in a skillet sprayed with butter-flavor nonstick cooking spray until tender. Add the tomatoes, water, broth, basil, curry powder and pepper and mix well. Bring to a boil; reduce heat. Simmer, covered, until the vegetables are tender, stirring occasionally. Stir in the rice. Cook for 20 minutes longer or until the rice is tender. Ladle into soup bowls. **Yield:** 4 servings.

Per Serving:
Calories: 101; Carbohydrate: 19.4 g; Protein: 3.3 g; Total Fat: 1.3 g;
Cholesterol: 0 mg; Sodium: 310 mg; Fiber: trace;
Calories from Fat: 12%

Beat the Clock

Steak Salad for Two

½ cup sliced fresh mushrooms
½ cup thinly sliced onion
6 ounces beef, sliced
1 clove of garlic, minced
Pepper to taste
2 tablespoons fat-free Italian salad dressing

Sauté the mushrooms and onion in a skillet sprayed with nonstick cooking spray. Transfer to a platter. Add the beef and garlic to the skillet. Sauté until the beef is of the desired degree of doneness. Sprinkle with the pepper. Stir in the mushroom mixture. Cook just until heated through. Serve over salad greens. Drizzle with the fat-free Italian salad dressing. **Yield:** 2 servings.

Per Serving:
Calories: 242; Carbohydrate: 6.6 g; Protein: 21.9 g; Total Fat: 7.5 g;
Cholesterol: 73.5 mg; Sodium: 65 mg; Fiber: trace;
Calories from Fat: 28%

Grilled Garlic Bagels

4 plain bagels, cut into halves
Minced garlic or garlic powder to taste
Grated fat-free Parmesan cheese to taste

Spray griddle or skillet with nonstick cooking spray. Spray cut side of bagels with butter-flavor nonstick cooking spray; sprinkle with garlic. Arrange cut side down on prepared griddle. Bake just until light brown; turn. Sprinkle with cheese. Serve immediately. **Yield:** 8 servings.

Per Serving:
Calories: 81; Carbohydrate: 16.4 g; Protein: 3.6 g; Total Fat: 0.7 g;
Cholesterol: 0 mg; Sodium: 99 mg; Fiber: trace;
Calories from Fat: 0%

Yogurt Brownies

1 package double fudge brownie mix
½ cup plain nonfat yogurt

Combine the brownie mix, yogurt and the amount of water specified on the package in a bowl and mix well; omit the eggs and oil. Spread in a baking pan sprayed with nonstick cooking spray. Bake using package directions or until the edges pull from the sides of the pan. Cool in pan on a wire rack. Cut into bars. The nutritional profile is based on a brownie mix using 2 eggs and ½ cup oil. **Yield:** 15 (1-brownie) servings.

Per Serving:
Calories: 173; Carbohydrate: 35.4 g; Protein: 1.6 g; Total Fat: 2.4 g;
Cholesterol: trace; Sodium: 144 mg; Fiber: trace;
Calories from Fat: 12.5%

Drink water or diluted energy-replacement drinks before, during, and after exercise. Thirst is a poor indicator of need. Water is needed for temperature regulation.

Beat the Clock

Menu

Greek Spinach Salad *page 64*
Broiled Orange Roughy *page 65*
Baked Potato
Whole Wheat Rolls
Gingerbread *page 66*

Greek Spinach Salad

4 cups loosely packed fresh spinach, stems removed
¾ cup cherry tomato halves
½ cup chopped green bell pepper
¼ cup sliced purple onion, separated into rings
1 ounce feta cheese, crumbled
2 tablespoons vinegar
1½ tablespoons cooking sherry
1 tablespoon water
¾ teaspoon oregano

Tear the spinach into bite-size pieces. Place in a large salad bowl. Add the cherry tomatoes, green pepper, purple onion and feta cheese, tossing gently. Pour a mixture of the vinegar, cooking sherry, water and oregano over the spinach mixture, tossing to coat. **Yield:** 4 (1-cup) servings.

Per Serving:
Calories: 50; Carbohydrate: 5.4 g; Protein: 3.3 g; Total Fat: 1.5 g;
Cholesterol: 5 mg; Sodium: 112 mg; Fiber: 2 g;
Calories from Fat: 27%

Broiled Orange Roughy

2 (4-ounce) orange roughy fillets
Pepper to taste
2 tablespoons orange juice
2 teaspoons melted margarine
Garlic powder to taste
Dillweed to taste
2 tablespoons dried bread crumbs

Spray a broiler rack with nonstick cooking spray. Pat the fillets dry with a paper towel. Sprinkle lightly on both sides with pepper. Arrange on the prepared broiler rack in a broiler pan. Combine the orange juice, margarine and garlic powder in a bowl and mix well. Drizzle over the fillets. Sprinkle generously with dillweed. Broil for 6 to 7 minutes or until the fish flakes easily. Sprinkle with the bread crumbs. Broil for 1 minute longer. Serve immediately.
Yield: 2 servings.

Per Serving:
Calories: 183; Carbohydrate: 6.2 g; Protein: 26 g; Total Fat: 5.2 g;
Cholesterol: 34 mg; Sodium: 186 mg; Fiber: trace;
Calories from Fat: 26%

The two things you most need for your exercise program are 1) a partner, and 2) a good pair of shoes. Partners provide motivation for one another.

Beat the Clock

GINGERBREAD

1 cup dark molasses
½ cup packed brown sugar
½ cup vegetable oil
1 teaspoon ginger
½ teaspoon cinnamon
½ teaspoon ground cloves
½ teaspoon nutmeg
1 cup boiling water
2½ cups flour
1 teaspoon baking soda
2 tablespoons hot water

Combine the molasses, brown sugar, oil, ginger, cinnamon, cloves and nutmeg in a bowl and mix well. Stir in the boiling water. Add the flour and mix well. Dissolve the baking soda in the hot water in a small bowl and mix well. Stir into the batter. Spoon into an 8x8-inch baking pan sprayed with nonstick cooking spray. Bake at 350 degrees for 30 minutes. Cut into 12 slices. Serve warm. **Yield:** 12 servings.

PER SERVING:
CALORIES: 265; CARBOHYDRATE: 43 g; PROTEIN: 3 g; TOTAL FAT: 9 g;
CHOLESTEROL: 0 mg; SODIUM: 89 mg; FIBER: trace;
CALORIES FROM FAT: 30%

BEAT THE CLOCK

Menu

Spinach Salad with Honey Mustard Dressing *page 67*
Angel Hair Pasta with Lemon and Garlic *page 68*
Grilled Garlic Bagels *page 62*
Frozen Yogurt
Fat-Free Oatmeal Raisin Chewies *page 69*

Spinach Salad with Honey Mustard Dressing

10 to 12 ounces fresh spinach ♦ ¼ cup honey
2 tablespoons white wine ♦ 1 tablespoon Dijon mustard
1 tablespoon canola oil ♦ 2 teaspoons poppy seeds (optional)
½ teaspoon Worcestershire sauce
1 cup thinly sliced fresh mushrooms ♦ ½ red onion, thinly sliced

Rinse the spinach in cold water; drain. Remove the tough stems from the spinach. Wrap in paper towels and place in a sealable plastic bag. Chill the spinach until ready to assemble the salad. Whisk the honey, white wine, Dijon mustard, canola oil, poppy seeds and Worcestershire sauce together in a bowl. Tear the spinach into bite-size pieces and place in a large salad bowl. Top with the mushrooms and red onion. Pour the dressing over the salad, tossing to coat. **Yield:** 6 servings.

PER SERVING:
CALORIES: 91; CARBOHYDRATE: 11.7 g; PROTEIN: 3 g; TOTAL FAT: 2.7 g;
CHOLESTEROL: 0 mg; SODIUM: 100 mg; FIBER: 3 g;
CALORIES FROM FAT: 24%

BEAT THE CLOCK

ANGEL HAIR PASTA WITH LEMON AND GARLIC

2 cloves of garlic, minced
1 teaspoon olive oil
½ cup dry white wine
1 cup chopped tomato
¼ cup fresh lemon juice
4 ounces spinach angel hair pasta
4 ounces semolina angel hair pasta
¼ cup chopped fresh basil
2 tablespoons freshly grated Parmesan cheese
Freshly ground pepper to taste

Bring a large saucepan of water to a boil over high heat and maintain at a boil. Sauté the garlic in the olive oil in a sauté pan over medium heat just until the garlic turns light brown. Remove from heat. Add the white wine. Cook for 1 to 2 minutes longer or until the wine has been reduced by ½, stirring constantly. Stir in the tomato and lemon juice. Remove from heat. Place the pasta in the boiling water. Boil for 30 to 60 seconds or until of the desired degree of doneness. Drain and place in a heated serving bowl. Add the basil, cheese, pepper and tomato mixture, tossing to mix. Serve immediately. **Yield:** 4 servings.

PER SERVING:
CALORIES: 279; CARBOHYDRATE: 46 g; PROTEIN: 9 g; TOTAL FAT: 3.1 g;
CHOLESTEROL: 2 mg; SODIUM: 54 mg; FIBER: 0.3 g;
CALORIES FROM FAT: 10%

Fat-Free Oatmeal Raisin Chewies

2 egg whites
3 tablespoons plus 1 teaspoon light applesauce
2 tablespoons light corn syrup
1 teaspoon vanilla extract
1½ cups quick-cooking oats
½ cup flour
½ cup sugar
1 teaspoon cinnamon
½ teaspoon salt
½ teaspoon baking powder
½ teaspoon baking soda
⅔ cup raisins

Spray a cookie sheet with nonstick cooking spray. Combine the egg whites, applesauce, corn syrup and vanilla in a bowl and mix well. Combine the oats, flour, sugar, cinnamon, salt, baking powder and baking soda in a bowl and mix well. Add to the egg white mixture and mix well. Stir in the raisins. Drop by heaping teaspoonfuls 2 inches apart onto the prepared cookie sheet. Bake at 375 degrees for 10 minutes or until firm. Remove to a wire rack to cool completely. **Yield:** 12 (1-cookie) servings.

Per Serving:
Calories: 134; Carbohydrate: 29 g; Protein: 3 g; Total Fat: 0 g;
Cholesterol: 0 mg; Sodium: 146 mg; Fiber: trace;
Calories from Fat: 0%

Beat the Clock

Menu

Spinach Salad *page 70*
Dijon-Glazed Chicken *page 71*
Rice
Steamed Baby Carrots
Whole Wheat Rolls
Fresh Fruit in Season
Fruit Dip *page 46*

Spinach Salad

8 ounces fresh spinach, torn into bite-size pieces
4 mushrooms, sliced
4 green onions, sliced
1 (11-ounce) can mandarin oranges, drained
6 tablespoons grated fat-free Parmesan cheese
2 tablespoons slivered almonds
¼ cup fat-free Italian salad dressing

Combine the spinach, mushrooms, green onions, mandarin oranges, cheese and almonds in a salad bowl and mix well. Drizzle with the salad dressing, tossing to coat. **Yield:** 6 servings.

Per Serving:
Calories: 71; Carbohydrate: 12 g; Protein: 4 g; Total Fat: 2 g;
Cholesterol: 0 mg; Sodium: 208 mg; Fiber: 2 g;
Calories from Fat: 20%

Beat the Clock

Dijon-Glazed Chicken

4 (4-ounce) chicken breast halves
2 tablespoons Dijon mustard
1 tablespoon brown sugar
1 tablespoon honey
1 teaspoon minced gingerroot

Skin and debone the chicken breasts. Rinse and pat dry. Combine the Dijon mustard, brown sugar, honey and gingerroot in a bowl and mix well. Arrange the chicken on a grill rack; brush with ½ of the Dijon mustard glaze. Grill over hot coals for 5 minutes; turn the chicken. Brush with the remaining glaze. Grill for 5 minutes longer or until the chicken is cooked through. May arrange the chicken in a baking pan and brush with ½ of the glaze. Bake, covered, at 375 degrees for 15 to 20 minutes or until cooked through, turning once and basting with the remaining glaze. Remove the cover and broil until golden brown. **Yield:** 4 servings.

Per Serving:
Calories: 179; Carbohydrate: 7.1 g; Protein: 26.2 g; Total Fat: 2.1 g;
Cholesterol: 66 mg; Sodium: 298 mg; Fiber: trace;
Calories from Fat: 10.5%

When buying ground chicken or turkey, read the label carefully. If it doesn't say that it is ground from just chicken meat or skinless, skin may be ground up with the meat and the fat may double.

Beat the Clock

Menu

Spinach Salad with Orange Dressing *page 72*
Pesto Pasta for Two *page 73* ◆ Italian Bread
Berries with Honey Yogurt Sour Cream Sauce *page 73*

Spinach Salad with Orange Dressing

6 navel oranges, chilled ◆ 4 cups trimmed spinach
1½ cups trimmed watercress
1 tablespoon pine nuts ◆ ⅓ cup minced shallots
2 cloves of garlic, minced ◆ 5 tablespoons white balsamic vinegar
2 teaspoons sherry vinegar ◆ Pepper to taste

Peel the oranges and remove the white pith. Separate the sections of the oranges from the membrane over a bowl to catch the juice; set the sections aside. Squeeze the juice from the membranes into the bowl and reserve. Combine the spinach and watercress in a bowl. Sauté the pine nuts in a sauté pan over medium heat for 6 minutes or until golden brown, shaking the pan occasionally. Transfer the pine nuts to a bowl. Add the shallots, garlic, balsamic vinegar, sherry vinegar and reserved orange juice to the sauté pan. Bring to a boil over low heat, stirring frequently. Stir in the pepper. Drizzle over the spinach mixture, tossing to coat. Top each serving with the orange sections; sprinkle with the pine nuts. **Yield:** 4 servings.

Per Serving:
Calories: 141; Carbohydrate: 30 g; Protein: 5.4 g; Total Fat: 2.2 g;
Cholesterol: 0 mg; Sodium: 53 mg; Fiber: 1.8 g;
Calories from Fat: 14%

Pesto Pasta for Two

1 teaspoon olive oil
2 teaspoons chopped fresh parsley
2 teaspoons chopped fresh oregano
2 teaspoons chopped fresh basil ◆ 2 cloves of garlic, minced
Pepper to taste
Juice of ½ lemon
2 cups cooked pasta of choice
Grated fat-free Parmesan cheese to taste

Heat the olive oil in a nonstick skillet until hot. Add the parsley, oregano, basil, garlic and pepper and mix well. Cook until heated through, stirring constantly. Stir in the lemon juice. Add the pasta and cheese, tossing to coat. Serve immediately. **Yield:** 2 servings.

Per Serving:
Calories: 250; Carbohydrate: 32 g; Protein: 5.5 g; Total Fat: 7.75 g;
Cholesterol: 0 mg; Sodium: 11.5 mg; Fiber: trace;
Calories from Fat: 28%

Berries with
Honey Yogurt Sour Cream Sauce

½ cup fat-free sour cream
½ cup plain nonfat yogurt ◆ ¼ cup honey, or to taste
10 cups assorted fresh berries

Combine the sour cream, yogurt and honey in a bowl and mix well. Spoon 1 cup berries in each of 10 dessert bowls. Top each serving with 2 tablespoons of the sauce.
Yield: 10 (1-cup berries, 2-tablespoons sauce) servings.

Per Serving:
Calories: 105; Carbohydrate: 24.7 g; Protein: 1 g; Total Fat: 0 g;
Cholesterol: 2.5 mg; Sodium: 20 mg; Fiber: trace;
Calories from Fat: 0%

Beat the Clock

DOWN TIME

Once upon a time, American families spent a significant amount of time together engaged in the activities necessary to put three meals a day on the table. Even if the "man of the house" was away at work each day, the evening meal was generally a time when everyone gathered together, dining at a pre-determined time. Family members set the table and washed the dishes, often spending time around the table talking long after the meal was finished. That type of family meal now seems as long ago and far away as cave dwellers roasting mastodon over an open fire. Today this is more likely to be the scenario: Mom has a meeting at school until after 7 p.m., Dad doesn't know how to prepare anything that isn't cooked on a grill, daughter Devon has softball practice, and son Evan works at the local supermarket bagging groceries after school. No one's home at dinnertime but Dad, and even the most enthusiastic grill master won't fire up the charcoal for one person.

Even though leisurely mealtime preparation is no longer the norm, there are times that families set aside to enjoy meals together, usually on the weekends. Many of these "down times" provide opportunities for socializing at meals since they are times for including extended family members or friends.

These recipes are for those times, which, although they are admittedly fewer than they used to be, are when cooking's a pleasure and the real aim is cookin' up quality time with friends and family.

An afternoon of relaxation in the 1890s. Inset: 1996, Radnor Lake Natural Area, a wildlife sanctuary and an eighty-five acre lake only seven miles from downtown Nashville.

Lasagna Then

1½ pounds ground beef
1 (12-ounce) can
tomato paste
½ cup chopped onion
¾ teaspoon salt
½ cup grated
Parmesan cheese
2 cups cottage cheese
32 ounces mozzarella
cheese, shredded
10 lasagna noodles

Per Serving:
Calories: 620;
Carbohydrate: 51 g;
Protein: 40 g;
Total Fat: 28 g;
Cholesterol: 99 mg;
Sodium: 611 mg;
Fiber: trace;
Calories from Fat: 41%

Down Time

Lasagna Now

1 (10-ounce) package frozen no-salt-added chopped spinach, thawed
8 ounces lasagna noodles
1 pound ground turkey (skin removed before grinding)
8 ounces fresh mushrooms, sliced ♦ ½ cup chopped onion
3 cloves of garlic, minced ♦ 3 cups no-salt-added tomato sauce
2 teaspoons basil ♦ ½ teaspoon oregano
Freshly ground pepper to taste ♦ 2 cups nonfat cottage cheese
¼ cup egg substitute ♦ ¼ cup grated fat-free Parmesan cheese
8 ounces part-skim mozzarella cheese, shredded

Squeeze the moisture from the spinach. Cook the lasagna noodles using package directions and omitting the salt; drain. Sauté the ground turkey, mushrooms, onion and garlic in a nonstick skillet over medium-high heat until the turkey is no longer pink; cover. Cook until the mushrooms have released their juices; remove the cover. Cook over high heat until the juices have evaporated, stirring frequently. Stir in the tomato sauce, basil, oregano and pepper. Combine the spinach, cottage cheese, egg substitute and Parmesan cheese in a bowl and mix well. Layer ⅓ of the noodles, ½ of the spinach mixture, ⅓ of the ground turkey mixture and ⅓ of the mozzarella cheese in a 9x13-inch baking dish sprayed with nonstick cooking spray. Repeat the layers. Top with the remaining noodles, turkey mixture and cheese. Bake, covered with foil, at 375 degrees for 35 to 40 minutes or until bubbly. **Yield:** 9 servings.

Per Serving:
Calories: 326; Carbohydrate: 32 g; Protein: 31 g; Total Fat: 8 g;
Cholesterol: 49 mg; Sodium: 411 mg; Fiber: trace;
Calories from Fat: 22%

Menu

Celestial Salad *page 77*
Pork Tenderloin with Maple-Mustard Sauce *page 78*
Candied Sweet Potatoes *page 37* ♦ Steamed Broccoli
Sourdough Bread ♦ Bavarian Apple Torte *page 79*

Celestial Salad

Salad Dressing
¼ cup sugar ♦ ¼ cup orange juice
2 tablespoons olive oil ♦ 2 tablespoons chopped fresh parsley
2 tablespoons red wine vinegar ♦ 1 teaspoon celery seeds
½ teaspoon dry mustard

Salad
1 head romaine, torn into bite-size pieces
1 (11-ounce) can mandarin oranges, drained
1 cup seedless grape halves ♦ ½ cup chopped green onions
½ cup sliced fresh mushrooms
¼ cup sliced almonds, toasted (optional)

For the salad dressing, combine the ingredients in a jar with a tightfitting lid, shaking to mix.

For the salad, combine the romaine, mandarin oranges, grapes, green onions, mushrooms and ½ of the almonds in a salad bowl and mix gently. Add the salad dressing just before serving, tossing to coat. Sprinkle with the remaining almonds. **Yield:** 8 servings.

PER SERVING:
CALORIES: 95; CARBOHYDRATE: 13.4 g; PROTEIN: 1 g; TOTAL FAT: 3 g;
CHOLESTEROL: 0 mg; SODIUM: 8 mg; FIBER: 2 g;
CALORIES FROM FAT: 28%

DOWN TIME

Pork Tenderloin with Maple Mustard Sauce

Sauce
⅓ cup pure maple syrup
2 tablespoons Dijon mustard
Pork Tenderloin
½ teaspoon nutmeg
½ teaspoon thyme, crushed
¼ teaspoon basil, crushed
¼ teaspoon ground red pepper
¼ teaspoon ground cloves
¼ teaspoon cinnamon
¼ teaspoon black pepper
⅛ teaspoon allspice
1 (12- to 16-ounce) pork tenderloin
3 bay leaves

For the sauce, whisk the maple syrup and Dijon mustard in a small bowl until blended. Serve at room temperature.

For the pork tenderloin, combine the nutmeg, thyme, basil, red pepper, cloves, cinnamon, black pepper and allspice in a small bowl and mix well. Sprinkle all sides of the tenderloin with the spice mixture; rub. Place the bay leaves along the bottom of the tenderloin. Marinate, wrapped in plastic wrap, for 2 hours or longer. Place the tenderloin on a rack in a shallow roasting pan. Spray the tenderloin with olive oil-flavor nonstick cooking spray. Insert a meat thermometer into the tenderloin. Roast at 425 degrees for 25 to 35 minutes or to 160 to 170 degrees on the meat thermometer. Discard the bay leaves. Place the tenderloin on a serving platter; slice diagonally across the grain. Serve with the sauce. **Yield:** 4 servings.

PER SERVING:
CALORIES: 259; CARBOHYDRATE: 17 g; PROTEIN: 33 g; TOTAL FAT: 6 g;
CHOLESTEROL: 106 mg; SODIUM: 112 mg; FIBER: trace;
CALORIES FROM FAT: 20%

DOWN TIME

Bavarian Apple Torte

⅓ cup sugar
⅓ cup unsalted margarine
¼ teaspoon vanilla extract
1 cup sifted flour
4 cups sliced peeled apples
8 ounces nonfat cream cheese
¼ cup sugar
Egg substitute equivalent to 1 egg
½ teaspoon grated lemon peel
¼ teaspoon vanilla extract
⅓ cup sugar
½ teaspoon cinnamon
2 tablespoons sliced almonds, toasted

Beat ⅓ cup sugar, margarine and ¼ teaspoon vanilla in a mixer bowl until creamy. Add the flour and mix well. Pat over the bottom and 1½ inches up the side of a 9-inch springform pan. Arrange the apples on a baking sheet. Bake, covered with foil, at 400 degrees for 15 minutes. Beat the cream cheese and ¼ cup sugar in a mixer bowl until blended. Add the egg substitute, lemon peel and ¼ teaspoon vanilla, beating until mixed. Spread evenly in the prepared springform pan; top with the apple slices. Place on a baking sheet. Bake at 400 degrees for 40 minutes or until the crust is brown. Cool slightly. Sprinkle with a mixture of ⅓ cup sugar and cinnamon. Top with the almonds.
Yield: 8 servings.

Per Serving:
Calories: 316; Carbohydrate: 56 g; Protein: 3.9 g; Total Fat: 9.7 g;
Cholesterol: 0.5 mg; Sodium: 31 mg; Fiber: 2.9 g;
Calories from Fat: 28%

Eating high-fiber foods (wheat bran, whole grains, oats, beans, carrots, apples, oranges) fills you up and leaves less room for high-fat foods.

Down Time

DOWN TIME

MENU

Grapefruit Salad *page 80*
Penne and Roasted Red Pepper Salad *page 81*
Grilled Marinated Chicken Breasts *page 82*
Steamed Asparagus Spears
Zucchini Bread *page 82*

GRAPEFRUIT SALAD

3 envelopes unflavored gelatin
¾ cup cold water
¼ cup cold orange juice
¾ cup sugar
1 cup boiling water
Sections of 5 large pink grapefruits, cut into halves
1 (14-ounce) can juice-pack crushed pineapple
¼ cup slivered almonds

Soften the gelatin in a mixture of the cold water and orange juice in a bowl. Dissolve the sugar in the boiling water in a bowl. Add the gelatin mixture and mix well. Chill until partially set. Fold in the grapefruit sections, undrained pineapple and almonds. Spoon into an 8x8-inch dish or a 6-cup mold. Chill for 3 hours or until set. Unmold onto a lettuce-lined platter or cut into 2½-inch squares. **Yield:** 9 servings.

PER SERVING:
CALORIES: 150; CARBOHYDRATE: 32 g; PROTEIN: 4 g; TOTAL FAT: 2 g;
CHOLESTEROL: 0 mg; SODIUM: 5 mg; FIBER: 2 g;
CALORIES FROM FAT: 12%

Penne and Roasted Red Pepper Salad

10 ounces penne or rotini
1 (7½-ounce) jar roasted red peppers, drained, chopped
¼ cup chopped fresh basil or parsley
3 tablespoons capers, rinsed
2 tablespoons balsamic vinegar
1½ tablespoons extra-virgin olive oil
2 scallions, finely chopped
2 cloves of garlic, finely chopped
Freshly ground black pepper to taste
Cayenne to taste
Fresh basil or parsley sprigs

Cook the pasta in boiling water in a saucepan for 6 to 8 minutes or until al dente. Drain and rinse with cold water. Transfer the pasta to a large bowl. Add the roasted red peppers, ¼ cup basil, capers, balsamic vinegar, olive oil, scallions and garlic and mix well. Season with black pepper and cayenne. Top with fresh basil or parsley sprigs.
Yield: 4 servings.

Per Serving:
Calories: 315; Carbohydrate: 56 g; Protein: 11 g; Total Fat: 6 g;
Cholesterol: 0 mg; Sodium: 195 mg; Fiber: 2 g;
Calories from Fat: 17%

Down Time

Grilled Marinated Chicken Breasts

6 boneless skinless chicken breast halves
½ cup packed brown sugar ♦ ¼ cup vinegar
3 tablespoons dry mustard ♦ Juice of 1 lime
Juice of ½ large lemon ♦ 3 medium cloves of garlic, mashed
¼ teaspoon salt ♦ 1 tablespoon olive oil ♦ Pepper to taste

Rinse the chicken and pat dry. Arrange in a shallow dish. Mix the remaining ingredients in a bowl. Pour over the chicken, turning to coat. Marinate, covered, for 8 to 10 hours, turning once. Let stand at room temperature for 1 hour; drain. Grill the chicken over hot coals for 4 to 8 minutes per side or until cooked through. **Yield:** 6 servings.

Per Serving:
Calories: 215; Carbohydrate: 14 g; Protein: 27 g; Total Fat: 5 g;
Cholesterol: 73 mg; Sodium: 163 mg; Fiber: trace;
Calories from Fat: 23%
Nutritional profile includes entire amount of marinade.

Zucchini Bread

3 cups flour ♦ 1½ cups sugar ♦ 1¼ teaspoons baking soda
1 teaspoon ginger ♦ 1 teaspoon cinnamon
1 teaspoon ground cloves ♦ ½ teaspoon salt
½ teaspoon baking powder ♦ 2 cups grated zucchini
¾ cup applesauce ♦ ¼ cup canola oil ♦ 3 egg whites
2 teaspoons vanilla extract

Mix the first 8 ingredients in a bowl. Stir in the zucchini, applesauce, oil, egg whites and vanilla. Spoon into two 5x9-inch loaf pans sprayed with nonstick cooking spray. Bake at 350 degrees for 1 hour. **Yield:** 30 (1-slice) servings.

Per Serving:
Calories: 110; Carbohydrate: 21.3 g; Protein: 1.8 g; Total Fat: 2.0 g;
Cholesterol: 0 mg; Sodium: 87 mg; Fiber: trace;
Calories from Fat: 16%

Down Time

Menu

Grilled Quesadillas with Salsa *page 83* or Layered Mexican Dip *page 84* ◆ Mexican Tortilla Soup *page 85* Bean Enchiladas *page 86* or Chicken Enchiladas *page 87* Spicy Mexican Rice *page 88* ◆ Frozen Vanilla Yogurt

Grilled Quesadillas with Salsa

¼ cup plain nonfat yogurt
2 tablespoons chopped tomato
1 tablespoon chopped onion
2 teaspoons minced fresh cilantro
½ teaspoon lemon juice
½ cup shredded low-fat Monterey Jack cheese
¼ cup shredded low-fat Colby cheese
4 (8-inch) fat-free flour tortillas
1½ tablespoons canned chopped green chiles

Mix the yogurt, tomato, onion, cilantro and lemon juice in a bowl. Chill, covered, for 2 hours or longer. Divide the cheeses evenly among the tortillas, arranging just off center of each. Top evenly with the chiles. Place the tortillas on a grill rack coated with nonstick cooking spray. Grill over medium-hot coals for 30 seconds or until the bottoms of the tortillas are brown; fold. Grill for 30 seconds longer or until the cheese melts. Cut each tortilla into 4 wedges. Serve each wedge with 1½ teaspoons of the salsa. **Yield:** 16 servings.

Per Serving:
Calories: 42; Carbohydrate: 6 g; Protein: 2 g; Total Fat: 1 g;
Cholesterol: 3 mg; Sodium: 44 mg; Fiber: trace;
Calories from Fat: 30%

Spicy Salsa

Try mixing three 14-ounce cans chopped tomatoes, 1 bunch chopped green onions, 8 ounces tomato sauce, 1 chopped white onion, 1 teaspoon minced garlic, 6 to 8 ounces chopped green chiles, 1¼ teaspoons minced cilantro, 1 to 2 finely chopped jalapeños and ¼ teaspoon oregano for another salsa variation. Store, covered, in the refrigerator for up to 2 weeks. The longer the salsa is stored the spicier the flavor.

Down Time

LAYERED MEXICAN DIP

1 large onion, chopped
3 tablespoons fat-free low-sodium chicken broth
8 ounces ground tenderloin breast of turkey, cooked, drained
2 (16-ounce) cans fat-free refried beans
1 (4-ounce) can chopped green chiles
3 cups shredded nonfat mozzarella cheese
1 cup shredded nonfat Cheddar cheese
2 cups fresh salsa
1 cup fat-free sour cream

Brown the onion in the broth in a skillet, stirring constantly. Stir in the ground turkey. Add the refried beans and mix well. Spread in a 9x13-inch baking dish sprayed with nonstick cooking spray. Sprinkle with the chiles. Sprinkle ½ of the mozzarella cheese and ½ of the Cheddar cheese over the prepared layers. Spread with the salsa. Top with the remaining mozzarella cheese and remaining Cheddar cheese. Bake at 400 degrees for 20 to 25 minutes or until bubbly. Cool slightly. Spread the sour cream in the shape of a cross over the top. Serve with low-fat tortilla chips or homemade low-fat chips.
Yield: 32 (¼-cup) servings.

PER SERVING:
CALORIES: 197; CARBOHYDRATE: 16.4 g; PROTEIN: 17.2 g; TOTAL FAT: 0.3 g;
CHOLESTEROL: 25 mg; SODIUM: 548 mg; FIBER: 6.5 g;
CALORIES FROM FAT: 1%

DOWN TIME

Mexican Tortilla Soup

1 medium onion, chopped
1 clove of garlic, chopped
1 jalapeño, seeded, minced
¼ teaspoon cayenne
2 medium tomatoes
3 cups low-sodium chicken broth
2 cups (8-ounces) shredded cooked chicken
2 teaspoons fresh lime juice
1 teaspoon grated lime zest
½ teaspoon salt
½ teaspoon freshly ground black pepper
2 teaspoons vegetable oil
4 (5½-inch) stale corn tortillas, cut into ¼-inch strips
½ cup (2 ounces) shredded low-fat Monterey Jack cheese

Spray a nonstick skillet with nonstick cooking spray. Add the onion, garlic and jalapeño to the prepared skillet. Sauté for 5 minutes or until the onion is tender. Stir in the cayenne. Cook for 1 minute, stirring constantly. Transfer the mixture to a food processor container. Arrange the tomatoes on a baking sheet lined with foil. Broil 6 inches from the heat source for 15 to 20 minutes or until charred, turning occasionally. Add the tomatoes to the food processor container. Process until puréed. Combine the tomato purée and broth in a saucepan. Bring to a boil; reduce heat. Simmer for 10 minutes, stirring occasionally. Stir in the chicken, lime juice, lime zest, salt and black pepper. Cook until heated through, stirring occasionally. Heat the oil in a nonstick skillet over medium-high heat. Add the tortilla strips. Cook for 8 to 10 minutes or until brown, turning frequently; drain. Ladle the soup into soup bowls. Top each serving with tortilla strips; sprinkle each serving with 2 tablespoons shredded cheese. **Yield:** 4 (1¼-cup) servings.

Per Serving:
Calories: 240; Carbohydrate: 20.6 g; Protein: 22 g; Total Fat: 8.1 g;
Cholesterol: 7.5 mg; Sodium: 347 mg; Fiber: 1.8 g;
Calories from Fat: 30%

Down Time

Bean Enchiladas

Tomato Chili Sauce
2 (8-ounce) cans no-salt-added tomato sauce
1 (4-ounce) can chopped green chiles
½ cup chopped green onions ♦ 2 teaspoons chili powder
½ teaspoon cumin ♦ ¼ teaspoon oregano
1 clove of garlic, minced

Enchiladas
1 (16-ounce) can fat-free refried beans
½ cup water ♦ 2 teaspoons chili powder
¼ teaspoon pepper ♦ ⅛ teaspoon garlic powder
12 (6-inch) corn, flour or whole wheat tortillas
1 cup shredded nonfat Cheddar cheese
¾ cup fat-free sour cream (optional)
Chopped green onions (optional)

For the sauce, combine the tomato sauce, undrained chiles, ¼ cup green onions, 2 teaspoons chili powder, cumin, oregano and garlic in a saucepan or microwave-safe dish. Cook or microwave until heated through, stirring occasionally.

For the enchiladas, combine the refried beans, water, 2 teaspoons chili powder, pepper, garlic powder and ½ cup of the tomato chili sauce in a bowl. Spread ⅓ cup of the refried bean mixture over the surface of each tortilla; roll loosely to enclose filling. Place seam side down in a 9x13-inch baking dish sprayed with nonstick cooking spray. Spoon the remaining tomato chili sauce over the enchiladas. Bake, covered, at 350 degrees for 20 minutes. Sprinkle with the cheese. Bake for 5 minutes longer or until the cheese melts. Top each enchilada with 1 tablespoon sour cream; sprinkle with green onions. If using corn tortillas, steam lightly over boiling water for approximately 2 minutes or until soft and pliable before spreading with the bean mixture. **Yield:** 12 (1-enchilada) servings.

Per Serving:
Calories: 165; Carbohydrate: 12.6 g; Protein: 6.5 g; Total Fat: 2 g;
Cholesterol: 0 mg; Sodium: 520 mg; Fiber: 3 g;
Calories from Fat: 11%

Chicken Enchiladas

1 tablespoon margarine
½ cup chopped onion
1 clove of garlic, minced
1 (10¾-ounce) can fat-free cream of chicken soup
1 (4-ounce) can diced green chiles, drained (optional)
½ cup fat-free sour cream
1½ cups chopped cooked skinless chicken breast
1 cup (4-ounces) shredded low-fat Cheddar cheese
10 fat-free flour tortillas, heated
¼ cup skim milk

Heat the margarine in a nonstick skillet until melted. Add the onion and garlic. Cook until tender, stirring constantly. Stir in the soup, chiles and sour cream. Remove from heat. Reserve ¾ cup of the sauce. Stir the chicken and ½ cup of the cheese into the remaining sauce. Fill the tortillas with the chicken mixture; roll to enclose the filling. Place seam side down in an ungreased 8x12-inch baking dish. Combine the reserved sauce and skim milk in a small bowl and mix well. Spoon over the enchiladas. Sprinkle with the remaining cheese. Bake at 350 degrees for 30 to 35 minutes or until bubbly.
Yield: 10 (1-enchilada) servings.

Per Serving:
Calories: 194; Carbohydrate: 22.4 g; Protein: 18 g; Total Fat: 4 g;
Cholesterol: 38.5 mg; Sodium: 475 mg; Fiber: trace;
Calories from Fat: 19%

Use low-fat and imitation cheese whenever possible instead of natural, processed, and hard cheeses that are higher in saturated fat.

Down Time

Physical stress may
be indicated by pounding
heart, increased blood
pressure, fatigue, or cold
or sweaty hands.
Emotional stress may be
manifested through
depression, anger,
irritability, or low
self-esteem. Behavioral
stress may surface
through overeating, an
increase in drinking or
smoking, or forgetfulness.

Down Time

Spicy Mexican Rice

⅔ cup long grain rice
⅓ cup chopped onion
⅓ cup chopped green bell pepper
1 cup chopped tomato
½ teaspoon chili powder
¼ teaspoon salt
¼ teaspoon garlic powder
¼ teaspoon ground red pepper
1⅓ cups canned no-salt-added beef broth

Spray a large nonstick skillet with nonstick cooking spray. Heat over medium-high heat until hot. Add the rice, onion and green pepper to the prepared skillet. Sauté until the vegetables are tender-crisp and light brown. Stir in the tomato, chili powder, salt, garlic powder, red pepper and broth. Bring to a boil; reduce heat. Simmer, covered, for 20 to 25 minutes or until the rice is tender and the liquid has been absorbed. **Yield:** 6 servings.

Per Serving:
Calories: 84; Carbohydrate: 18.4 g; Protein: 3 g; Total Fat: trace;
Cholesterol: 0 mg; Sodium: 115 mg; Fiber: 0.5 g;
Calories from Fat: 1%

Menu

Baked Fish *page 89*
Steamed Rice
Oven-Roasted Vegetables *page 90*
with Broccoli Pesto *page 91*
Sun-Dried Tomato Bread
Strawberry Angel Food Delight *page 91*

Baked Fish

2 lemons, thinly sliced
1 pound fish fillets of choice (salmon, halibut, sole, catfish)
½ cup fat-free sour cream
Chopped green onions to taste
Chopped fresh parsley to taste
Paprika to taste

Line the bottom of a baking dish with lemon slices. Spray the fillets with olive oil-flavor nonstick cooking spray. Arrange on top of the lemon slices. Bake, covered, at 350 degrees for 20 minutes or until the fish flakes easily. Spread with the sour cream. Bake just until heated. Sprinkle with green onions, parsley and paprika.
Yield: 4 servings.

Per Serving:
Calories: 173; Carbohydrate: 9.2 g; Protein: 24.5 g; Total Fat: 3.4 g;
Cholesterol: 53 mg; Sodium: 110 mg; Fiber: trace;
Calories from Fat: 17%

Down Time

Oven-Roasted Vegetables

4 medium tomatoes, thinly sliced
4 medium zucchini, thinly sliced
4 medium red onions, thinly sliced
2 medium eggplant, thinly sliced
¼ cup Broccoli Pesto (page 91)
¼ cup finely minced garlic
Freshly ground pepper to taste
¼ cup chopped fresh thyme
1 cup chopped fresh Italian parsley

Arrange the tomatoes, zucchini, red onions and eggplant in rows in a single layer on 2 baking sheets. Combine the pesto, garlic and pepper in a bowl and mix well. Spoon the pesto mixture over the vegetables. Sprinkle with the thyme and parsley. Spray the vegetables lightly with olive oil-flavor nonstick cooking spray. Bake at 400 degrees for 35 to 40 minutes. Broil until lightly charred. Serve immediately. **Yield:** 8 servings.

Per Serving:
Calories: 35; Carbohydrate: 7 g; Protein: 2 g; Total Fat: 1 g;
Cholesterol: 0 mg; Sodium: 35 mg; Fiber: trace;
Calories from Fat: 11%

Down Time

Broccoli Pesto

4 cups chopped broccoli florets ♦ 1 cup low-sodium chicken broth
4 cloves of garlic ♦ 1 cup packed fresh basil leaves
¼ cup grated fat-free Parmesan cheese
⅛ teaspoon salt

Steam the broccoli over the broth in a large saucepan for 5 minutes or until tender. Transfer the broccoli to a bowl and reserve the liquid. Add additional chicken broth to the reserved liquid to measure 6 tablespoons. Process the garlic in a food processor until minced; scrape the side of the work bowl. Add the basil. Process until finely chopped. Add 2 tablespoons of the reserved liquid. Process until smooth. Add the broccoli, cheese, salt and remaining reserved liquid. Process until smooth, scraping the side frequently. Store, covered, in the refrigerator until needed. **Yield:** 9 (¼-cup) servings.

Per Serving:
Calories: 28; Carbohydrate: 3 g; Protein: 2.8 g; Total Fat: 0.3 g;
Cholesterol: trace; Sodium: 93 mg; Fiber: trace;
Calories from Fat: 9%

Strawberry Angel Food Delight

1 angel food cake
2 (4-ounce) packages sugar-free vanilla instant pudding mix
3 cups fresh strawberries ♦ 1 cup light whipped topping

Cut the angel food cake into 1½-inch cubes. Prepare the pudding mix following package directions using skim milk. Layer the angel food cake, pudding and strawberries ½ at a time in a trifle bowl or large serving bowl. Spread with the whipped topping.
Yield: 12 servings.

Per Serving:
Calories: 177; Carbohydrate: 36.7 g; Protein: 5.6 g; Total Fat: 0.6 g;
Cholesterol: 0 mg; Sodium: 350 mg; Fiber: trace;
Calories from Fat: 3%

Down Time

Menu

Fresh Vegetables with Easy Nonfat Yogurt Dip *page 45*
Low-Fat Original Chex Mix *page 92*
or Hot and Spicy Low-Fat Chex Mix *page 93*
Gazpacho *page 93* ♦ Fast Fall Fruit Salad *page 94*
Pasta Salad *page 94*
Crispy Baked Chicken *page 95*
Sourdough Bread ♦ Yogurt Brownies *page 63*

Low-Fat Original Chex Mix

8 cups Chex cereal (rice, wheat, corn or any combination)
½ cup unsalted pretzels (optional)
1 tablespoon reduced-calorie margarine
4½ teaspoons Worcestershire sauce
1½ teaspoons seasoned salt

Spray a large baking pan with butter-flavor nonstick cooking spray. Combine the cereal and pretzels in a bowl and toss lightly. Heat the margarine in a saucepan until melted. Stir in the Worcestershire sauce and seasoned salt. Pour over the cereal mixture, tossing to coat. Spoon into the prepared baking pan. Bake at 250 degrees for 45 minutes, stirring occasionally. **Yield:** 16 (½-cup) servings.

Per Serving:
Calories: 83; Carbohydrate: 2.2 g; Protein: 1.7 g; Total Fat: 0.7 g;
Cholesterol: 0 mg; Sodium: 212.8 mg; Fiber: trace;
Calories from Fat: 8%

DOWN TIME

Hot and Spicy Low-Fat Chex Mix

8 cups rice or corn Chex cereal ♦ ¼ cup red hot cinnamon candies
1 tablespoon reduced-fat margarine ♦ ½ teaspoon onion powder
½ teaspoon garlic powder ♦ ¼ to ½ teaspoon cayenne

Spray a large baking pan with butter-flavor nonstick cooking spray. Toss the cereal and candies in a bowl. Melt the margarine in a saucepan. Stir in the seasonings. Pour over the cereal mixture; toss to coat. Spoon into the prepared baking pan. Bake at 250 degrees for 45 minutes, stirring occasionally. **Yield:** 16 (½-cup) servings.

PER SERVING:
CALORIES: 73; CARBOHYDRATE: 16 g; PROTEIN: 1.4 g; TOTAL FAT: 0.7 g;
CHOLESTEROL: 0 mg; SODIUM: 143 mg; FIBER: trace;
CALORIES FROM FAT: 9%

Gazpacho

3 to 6 tomatoes, seeded, cut into quarters
1 medium green bell pepper, cut into quarters
1 medium cucumber, peeled, seeded, cut into quarters
1 small onion, cut into wedges
1 small jalapeño, seeded, cut into quarters
2 cloves of garlic, cut into halves
2 tablespoons lime juice or lemon juice ♦ 2 tablespoons vinegar
1 tablespoon olive oil ♦ 1 teaspoon grated lime peel
3 cups tomato juice ♦ ⅛ teaspoon ground red pepper

Combine the the first 10 ingredients in a food processor or blender container. Process until smooth. Pour into a large bowl. Stir in the tomato juice and red pepper. Chill, covered, until serving time. Ladle into soup bowls. **Yield:** 6 (1-cup) servings.

PER SERVING:
CALORIES: 63; CARBOHYDRATE: 14.3 g; PROTEIN: 2.3 g; TOTAL FAT: 2 g;
CHOLESTEROL: 0 mg; SODIUM: 207 mg; FIBER: trace;
CALORIES FROM FAT: 28%

Lemons give more juice at room temperature. Heat chilled lemons in hot water for 10 to 15 seconds. Always roll lemons on the counter before juicing to get more liquid.

DOWN TIME

Fast Fall Fruit Salad

1 (16-ounce) package frozen peach slices
1 (16-ounce) package frozen red raspberries
1 (16-ounce) package frozen blueberries
1 (10-ounce) package frozen strawberry halves
¼ cup sugar

Combine the peaches, raspberries, blueberries and strawberries in a bowl. Add the sugar and mix lightly. Let stand at room temperature for 30 minutes. Serve immediately. In the summer fresh fruit may be substituted for the frozen fruit, but chill the fruit before serving rather than allowing to sit at room temperature. **Yield:** 6 servings.

Per Serving:
Calories: 111; Carbohydrate: 28 g; Protein: 1.2 g; Total Fat: 0.5 g;
Cholesterol: 0 mg; Sodium: 3.8 mg; Fiber: 2.2 g;
Calories from Fat: 4%

Pasta Salad

16 ounces tricolor rotini
Florets of 1 bunch broccoli, steamed
4 carrots, sliced, steamed
1 pint cherry tomatoes, cut into halves
4 ounces feta cheese, crumbled
1 (8-ounce) bottle fat-free Caesar salad dressing

Cook the pasta using package directions. Rinse and drain. Combine the pasta, broccoli, carrots and cherry tomatoes in a bowl and mix lightly. Stir in the feta cheese. Add the salad dressing, tossing to coat. **Yield:** 10 servings.

Per Serving:
Calories: 227; Carbohydrate: 40 g; Protein: 8 g; Total Fat: 3.4 g;
Cholesterol: 10 mg; Sodium: 375 mg; Fiber: 2.4 g;
Calories from Fat: 14%

Down Time

CRISPY BAKED CHICKEN

1 (2½- to 3-pound) chicken, cut up, skinned
1 cup skim milk
1 cup cornflake crumbs
1 teaspoon rosemary
½ teaspoon paprika
½ teaspoon freshly ground pepper

Line a baking pan with foil; spray lightly with nonstick cooking spray. Rinse the chicken and pat dry. Trim any visible fat. Pour the skim milk into a shallow bowl. Combine the cornflake crumbs, rosemary, paprika and pepper in a shallow bowl and mix well. Dip the chicken in the skim milk; roll in the cornflake mixture. Let stand briefly to allow coating to adhere. Arrange the chicken with pieces not touching in the prepared pan. Bake at 400 degrees for 45 minutes or until cooked through. **Yield:** 4 servings.

PER SERVING:
CALORIES: 249; CARBOHYDRATE: 12 g; PROTEIN: 32 g; TOTAL FAT: 7 g;
CHOLESTEROL: 92 mg; SODIUM: 142 mg; FIBER: trace;
CALORIES FROM FAT: 25%

Plan menus ahead of time. Make a shopping list based on these menus and shop from your list. Eat before you shop to avoid impulsive buying.

DOWN TIME

On the Go

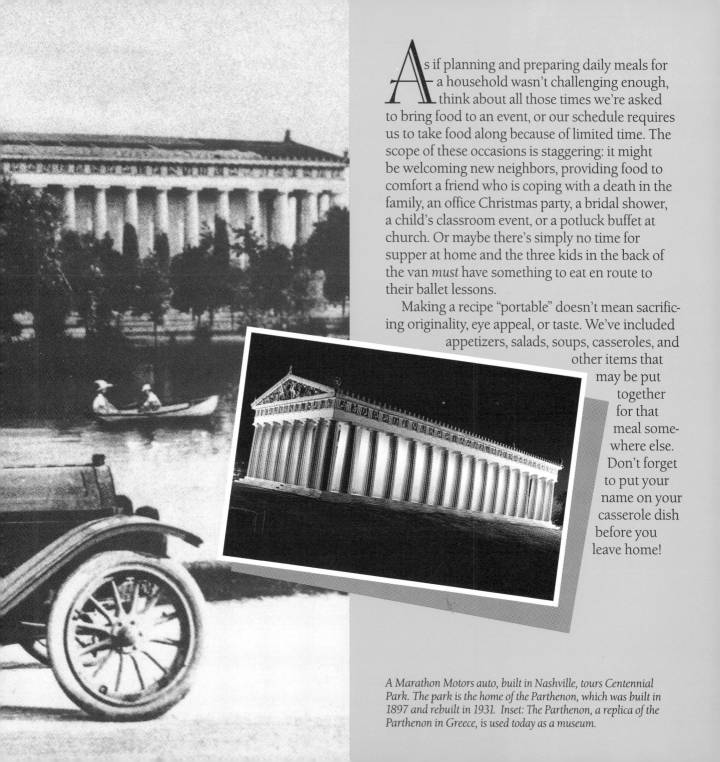

As if planning and preparing daily meals for a household wasn't challenging enough, think about all those times we're asked to bring food to an event, or our schedule requires us to take food along because of limited time. The scope of these occasions is staggering: it might be welcoming new neighbors, providing food to comfort a friend who is coping with a death in the family, an office Christmas party, a bridal shower, a child's classroom event, or a potluck buffet at church. Or maybe there's simply no time for supper at home and the three kids in the back of the van *must* have something to eat en route to their ballet lessons.

Making a recipe "portable" doesn't mean sacrificing originality, eye appeal, or taste. We've included appetizers, salads, soups, casseroles, and other items that may be put together for that meal somewhere else. Don't forget to put your name on your casserole dish before you leave home!

A Marathon Motors auto, built in Nashville, tours Centennial Park. The park is the home of the Parthenon, which was built in 1897 and rebuilt in 1931. Inset: The Parthenon, a replica of the Parthenon in Greece, is used today as a museum.

Squash Casserole Then

2 pounds yellow
squash, sliced
2 carrots, grated
1 large onion, chopped
1 (10-ounce) can cream of
chicken soup
1 cup sour cream
1 package corn bread
stuffing
½ cup butter
1 (8-ounce) can water
chestnuts

Per Serving:
Calories: 308;
Carbohydrate: 29 g;
Protein: 5 g;
Total Fat: 19 g;
Cholesterol: 43 mg;
Sodium: 427 mg;
Fiber: trace;
Calories from Fat: 56%

On the Go

Squash Casserole Now

2 pounds yellow squash, sliced
2 carrots, grated
1 (10-ounce) can low-fat low-sodium cream of chicken soup
1 cup fat-free sour cream
1 (8-ounce) package corn bread stuffing

Combine the squash and carrots with enough water to cover in a saucepan. Cook until tender; drain. Combine the squash mixture, soup and sour cream in a bowl and mix well. Layer the squash mixture and corn bread stuffing ½ at a time in a baking dish, spraying the stuffing layers with fat-free spray margarine. Bake at 350 degrees for 45 minutes. **Yield:** 12 servings.

Per Serving:
Calories: 115; Carbohydrate: 22.6 g; Protein: 3.3 g; Total Fat: 1.4 g;
Cholesterol: 5.1 mg; Sodium: 328 mg; Fiber: trace;
Calories from Fat: 11%

Baked Artichoke Dip

1 (14-ounce) can artichoke hearts, drained, chopped
¾ cup fat-free mayonnaise
1 cup grated fat-free Parmesan cheese
1 clove of garlic, minced
¼ teaspoon Worcestershire sauce
Hot sauce to taste

Combine the artichokes, mayonnaise, cheese, garlic, Worcestershire sauce and hot sauce in a bowl and mix well. Spoon into a 1-quart baking dish sprayed lightly with nonstick cooking spray. Bake at 350 degrees for 20 minutes or until bubbly. Serve with party crackers. **Yield:** 24 (2-tablespoon) servings.

Per Serving:
Calories: 27; Carbohydrate: 5.7 g; Protein: 1.4 g; Total Fat: trace; Cholesterol: 0 mg; Sodium: 154 mg; Fiber: trace; Calories from Fat: 0%

Hummus

1 (15-ounce) can chick-peas
⅓ cup lemon juice
3 tablespoons tahini ♦ 2 cloves of garlic
Chopped fresh parsley to taste
Red pepper to taste

Drain the chick-peas, reserving 1 to 2 tablespoons of the chick-peas. Process the remaining chick-peas, lemon juice, tahini and garlic in a food processor until smooth. Spoon onto a platter. Top with the reserved chick-peas; sprinkle with parsley and red pepper. Serve with pita bread or toasted pita chips. **Yield:** 8 (¼-cup) servings.

Per Serving:
Calories: 108; Carbohydrate: 15 g; Protein: 4 g; Total Fat: 4 g; Cholesterol: 0 mg; Sodium: 186 mg; Fiber: 3.5 g; Calories from Fat: 30%

On the Go

Spinach Cheddar Squares

1 (10-ounce) package frozen chopped spinach, thawed
¼ cup dry bread crumbs
¾ cup shredded low-fat Cheddar cheese
1½ cups egg substitute
¾ cup skim milk
¼ cup chopped fresh roasted red bell pepper (optional)
1 tablespoon dried onion flakes
1 tablespoon grated fat-free Parmesan cheese
⅛ teaspoon garlic powder
⅛ teaspoon pepper

Squeeze moisture from the spinach. Sprinkle the bread crumbs evenly over the bottom of an 8x8-inch baking dish lightly coated with canola oil. Layer ½ cup of the Cheddar cheese and the spinach over the bread crumbs. Combine the egg substitute, skim milk, red pepper, onion flakes, Parmesan cheese, garlic powder and pepper in a bowl and mix well. Pour over the prepared layers; sprinkle with the remaining Cheddar cheese. Bake at 350 degrees for 35 to 40 minutes or until bubbly. Let stand for 10 minutes. Cut into 2-inch squares. Serve immediately. **Yield:** 16 (2-inch square) servings.

PER SERVING:
CALORIES: 34.6; CARBOHYDRATE: 2.0 g; PROTEIN: 4 g; TOTAL FAT: 1.0 g;
CHOLESTEROL: 2 mg; SODIUM: 100 mg; FIBER: trace;
CALORIES FROM FAT: 26%

On the Go

Black Bean Soup

1½ cups dried black beans
2 quarts low-sodium chicken broth
1 lemon, cut into thick slices
½ cup minced onion
2 cloves of garlic, minced
⅛ teaspoon cumin
¼ cup chopped sun-dried tomatoes
⅛ teaspoon crushed red pepper
1 teaspoon crushed oregano
1 teaspoon crushed basil
1 teaspoon chopped seeded jalapeño
1 teaspoon marjoram
1 tablespoon sherry wine vinegar (optional)

Rinse and sort the black beans. Combine the beans with enough water to cover by 3 inches in a bowl. Let stand for 8 to 10 hours; drain. Combine the beans, broth and lemon slices in a stockpot. Simmer until the beans are tender, stirring occasionally. Sauté the onion, garlic and cumin in a nonstick skillet until tender and the mixture produces a good aroma. Stir the sautéed onion mixture, sun-dried tomatoes, red pepper, oregano, basil, jalapeño and marjoram into the beans. Simmer for 15 minutes longer, stirring occasionally. Discard the lemon slices. Process ⅓ of the bean mixture in a food processor until puréed. Return the purée to the stockpot. Stir in the vinegar. Simmer just until heated through. Ladle into soup bowls. May be frozen for future use. Yield: 10 servings.

Per Serving:
Calories: 150; Carbohydrate: 22 g; Protein: 10 g; Total Fat: 2 g;
Cholesterol: 10 mg; Sodium: 20 mg; Fiber: trace;
Calories from Fat: 12%

On the Go

LENTIL SOUP

2 cups dried lentils
7 cups water
4 medium carrots, chopped
3 ribs celery, chopped
1 medium onion, chopped
1½ teaspoons minced garlic
1 (16-ounce) can tomato sauce
1 tomato, chopped
Juice of ½ lemon
2 tablespoons white wine vinegar
1 tablespoon low-sodium soy sauce
1½ tablespoons brown sugar
1½ teaspoons basil
¼ teaspoon pepper
Grated fat-free Parmesan cheese (optional)

Sort and rinse the lentils. Combine the lentils, water, carrots, celery, onion and garlic in a stockpot. Simmer, covered, for 1½ hours, stirring occasionally. Add the tomato sauce, tomato, lemon juice, wine vinegar, soy sauce, brown sugar, basil and pepper and mix well. Simmer, covered, for 30 minutes longer, stirring occasionally. Add additional water for a thinner consistency if desired. Ladle into soup bowls; sprinkle with Parmesan cheese. **Yield:** 8 servings.

PER SERVING:
CALORIES: 198; CARBOHYDRATE: 34 g; PROTEIN: 14 g; TOTAL FAT: 1 g;
CHOLESTEROL: 0 mg; SODIUM: 402 mg; FIBER: 8 g;
CALORIES FROM FAT: 3%

Low-Fat Low-Sodium Vegetable Soup

1 (10-ounce) package frozen fordhook lima beans
1 (9-ounce) package frozen cut green beans
18 cups water
⅓ cup parsley flakes
6 tablespoons (rounded) low-sodium beef bouillon
1 tablespoon Lawry's Salt-Free 17 Seasoning
½ teaspoon garlic powder
2 (14½-ounce) cans no-salt-added whole tomatoes, chopped
1 bunch celery with leaves, chopped
1 large onion, chopped
2 cups chopped carrots
3 medium potatoes, chopped
¼ head cabbage, shredded
3 tablespoons pearl barley
Sliced fresh mushrooms (optional)

Rinse the lima beans and green beans in hot water and drain. Combine the water, parsley flakes, bouillon, Salt-Free 17 Seasoning, garlic powder and undrained tomatoes in a stockpot and mix well. Bring to a boil. Stir in the lima beans, green beans, celery, onion, carrots, potatoes, cabbage, barley and mushrooms. Bring to a boil; reduce heat. Cook over medium to medium-low heat for 2 to 2½ hours or until of the desired consistency, stirring occasionally. Ladle into soup bowls. **Yield:** 12 servings.

Per Serving:
Calories: 113; Carbohydrate: 22 g; Protein: 3.8 g; Total Fat: trace;
Cholesterol: 0 mg; Sodium: 49 mg; Fiber: 3 g;
Calories from Fat: 1%

On the Go

Orange-Apricot Freeze Salad

2 cups fat-free plain yogurt
½ cup fresh orange juice ♦ ½ cup sugar
1 (17-ounce) can unpeeled apricot halves, drained, chopped
¼ cup coarsely chopped pecans

Mix the yogurt and orange juice in a bowl. Stir in the sugar, apricots and pecans. Spoon into 3-ounce paper cups. Freeze, covered, until set. Peel off the paper; slice. Serve on lettuce-lined salad plates. Garnish with fresh strawberries. **Yield:** 12 servings.

Per Serving:
Calories: 82; Carbohydrate: 15 g; Protein: 3 g; Total Fat: 1.6 g;
Cholesterol: trace; Sodium: 29 mg; Fiber: trace;
Calories from Fat: 18%

Vegetable Salad

1 (16-ounce) can seasoned green beans, drained
1 (16-ounce) can tiny peas, drained
1 (8-ounce) can water chestnuts, drained, sliced
1 (16-ounce) can Chinese vegetables ♦ 1 purple onion, thinly sliced
1½ cups chopped celery ♦ ¾ cup sugar ♦ ¾ cup vinegar
⅛ teaspoon salt ♦ Pepper to taste

Combine the first 6 ingredients in a bowl and mix gently. Combine the sugar, vinegar, salt and pepper in a saucepan and mix well. Cook over medium heat until the sugar dissolves, stirring frequently; do not boil. Let stand until cool. Pour over the green bean mixture, tossing to coat. Chill, covered, for 8 to 10 hours. **Yield:** 20 servings.

Per Serving:
Calories: 62; Carbohydrate: 13 g; Protein: 2 g; Total Fat: 1 g;
Cholesterol: 0 mg; Sodium: 85 mg; Fiber: 1 g;
Calories from Fat: 13%
Nutritional profile includes the entire amount of marinade.

On the Go

104

Black Bean Salad

Dressing
¼ cup balsamic vinegar
1 tablespoon chopped fresh cilantro
1 teaspoon cumin
½ teaspoon coriander
Freshly ground pepper to taste
2 tablespoons olive oil

Salad
1 pound dried black beans
11 cups cold water
1 teaspoon cumin
¼ teaspoon salt
2 cups fresh or frozen corn, cooked
1 green bell pepper, coarsely chopped
1 red bell pepper, coarsely chopped
1 medium purple onion, finely chopped

For the dressing, combine the balsamic vinegar, cilantro, 1 teaspoon cumin, coriander and pepper in a jar with a tightfitting lid and shake until mixed. Add the olive oil. Shake until mixed.

For the salad, sort and rinse the beans. Combine the beans with 8 cups of the cold water in a stockpot. Let stand for 8 to 10 hours. Drain and rinse thoroughly. Return the beans to the stockpot. Add the remaining 3 cups cold water, 1 teaspoon cumin and salt. Bring to a boil; reduce heat. Simmer for 45 minutes or just until tender. Remove from heat. Let stand until cool. Drain excess liquid. Combine the beans, corn, green pepper, red pepper and onion in a bowl and mix well. Add the dressing, tossing to coat. Chill, covered, for 2 to 10 hours. May store, covered, in the refrigerator for up to 3 days. May substitute 4 cups rinsed canned black beans for the dried black beans, omitting the salt. **Yield:** 8 large salads.

Per Serving:
Calories: 236; Carbohydrate: 30.4 g; Protein: 12 g; Total Fat: 4.4 g;
Cholesterol: 0 mg; Sodium: 65 mg; Fiber: 11.6 g;
Calories from Fat: 16%

Try pasta, rice, and dried peas and beans as main dishes and in casseroles, soups, or other one-dish meals with low-fat sauces.

On the Go

Marinated Black-Eyed Pea Salad

1½ cups water
1 medium white onion, cut into halves
½ teaspoon crushed red pepper
¼ teaspoon salt
⅛ teaspoon hickory-flavor liquid smoke
1 (16-ounce) package frozen black-eyed peas
½ cup raspberry wine vinegar
¼ cup water
3 tablespoons chopped fresh parsley
1 clove of garlic, minced
1 teaspoon olive oil
¼ teaspoon freshly ground black pepper
½ cup chopped red bell pepper
⅓ cup sliced purple onion, separated into rings

Combine 1½ cups water, 1 white onion, red pepper, salt and liquid smoke in a medium saucepan. Bring to a boil. Stir in the peas. Bring to a boil; reduce heat. Simmer, covered, for 40 to 45 minutes or until the peas are tender. Drain and discard the onion. Rinse the peas with cold water; drain. Transfer to a bowl. Combine the raspberry wine vinegar, ¼ cup water, parsley, garlic, olive oil, black pepper and red bell pepper in a bowl and mix well. Pour over the peas, tossing to coat. Marinate, covered, in the refrigerator for 8 hours, stirring occasionally. Stir in the purple onion. Spoon onto lettuce-lined plates using a slotted spoon. **Yield:** 5 servings.

Per Serving:
Calories: 154; Carbohydrate: 27.8 g; Protein: 8.6 g; Total Fat: 1.2 g;
Cholesterol: 0 mg; Sodium: 93 mg; Fiber: trace;
Calories from Fat: 7%
Nutritional profile includes the entire amount of marinade.

On the Go

Chicken Potpie

1 pound boneless skinless chicken breasts
1 cup peas
1 cup chopped carrot
1 cup chopped potato
1 onion, chopped
1 (14½-ounce) can fat-free low-sodium chicken broth
1½ cups skim milk
½ cup flour
Pepper to taste
1 cup flour
2 teaspoons baking powder
¼ teaspoon salt
½ cup skim milk
2 tablespoons reduced-calorie margarine

Rinse the chicken. Combine the chicken with enough water to cover in a saucepan. Bring to a boil. Boil until cooked through; drain. Chop the chicken. Steam the peas, carrot, potato and onion in a steamer until tender. Heat the broth in a saucepan over medium heat until hot. Whisk in 1½ cups skim milk, ½ cup flour and pepper until smooth. Cook until thickened, stirring constantly. Stir in the chicken, peas, carrot, potato and onion. Cook just until heated through. Spoon into a baking dish. Combine 1 cup flour, baking powder and salt in a bowl and mix well. Stir in ½ cup skim milk and margarine, stirring just until moistened. Drop by tablespoonfuls over the chicken mixture. Bake, covered, at 400 degrees for 15 minutes; remove cover. Bake for 10 minutes longer. **Yield:** 6 servings.

Per Serving:
Calories: 308; Carbohydrate: 38 g; Protein: 27 g; Total Fat: 4.8 g;
Cholesterol: 48 mg; Sodium: 383 mg; Fiber: trace;
Calories from Fat: 14%

A simple way to measure your fitness level is by counting your heart rate while at rest. As you get in better shape, the number will go down.

On the Go

Use less meat than the recipe calls for when making spaghetti sauce, chili, soups, or stews. Instead, add extra beans, onions, tomatoes, bell peppers, etc., for flavor and texture.

BLACK BEAN CHICKEN CHILI

1 tablespoon vegetable oil
1 large onion, chopped (1 cup)
1 medium green bell pepper, chopped
3 cloves of garlic, minced
1 fresh jalapeño, seeded, minced
2 tablespoons chili powder
1 teaspoon cumin
½ teaspoon oregano
½ teaspoon cayenne
3 cups (12-ounces) chopped cooked chicken
2 cups low-sodium canned crushed tomatoes
1½ cups no-salt-added chicken broth
1 cup chili sauce
2 teaspoons Worcestershire sauce
½ teaspoon black pepper
1 (16-ounce) can black beans, rinsed, drained
¾ cup plain nonfat yogurt
½ cup chopped red onion

Heat the oil in a stockpot over medium heat until hot. Add 1 onion, green pepper, garlic and jalapeño. Cook for 5 to 7 minutes or until tender, stirring frequently. Stir in the chili powder, cumin, oregano and cayenne. Cook for 1 minute, stirring constantly. Add the chicken, tomatoes, broth, chili sauce, Worcestershire sauce and pepper. Bring to a boil; reduce heat. Simmer, covered, for 15 minutes, stirring occasionally. Stir in the black beans. Cook, covered, for 5 minutes longer, stirring occasionally. Ladle into chili bowls. Top each serving with yogurt and sprinkle with chopped red onion.
Yield: 8 servings.

PER SERVING:
CALORIES: 187; CARBOHYDRATE: 25 g; PROTEIN: 17 g; TOTAL FAT: 3.8 g;
CHOLESTEROL: 0.5 mg; SODIUM: 477 mg; FIBER: 2.7 g;
CALORIES FROM FAT: 18%

Meatless Chili

2 tablespoons olive oil
1½ cups chopped onions
3 cloves of garlic, minced
2 tablespoons chili powder
½ teaspoon cumin
1 cup chopped carrot
1 green bell pepper, chopped
2 (14½-ounce) cans no-salt-added tomatoes
1 (16-ounce) can chick-peas, drained
1 (15-ounce) can kidney beans, drained
1 (10-ounce) package frozen corn, thawed
1 or 2 pickled jalapeños, chopped

Heat the olive oil in a 5-quart saucepan over medium heat until hot. Add the onions, garlic, chili powder and cumin. Sauté for 5 minutes or until the onions and garlic are tender. Stir in the carrot and green pepper. Sauté for 2 minutes. Add the undrained tomatoes; crush with a spoon. Stir in the chick-peas, kidney beans, corn and jalapeños. Bring to a boil; reduce heat. Simmer, covered, for 30 to 35 minutes or until of the desired consistency, stirring occasionally. Ladle into chili bowls. May serve over rice. **Yield:** 8 (1½-cup) servings.

Per Serving:
Calories: 260; Carbohydrate: 42 g; Protein: 12 g; Total Fat: 3.5 g;
Cholesterol: 0 mg; Sodium: 360 mg; Fiber: trace;
Calories from Fat: 12%

On the Go

Shrimp and Scallop Stroganoff

1 low-sodium chicken bouillon cube
1 cup hot water
1 pound large shrimp
1 pound sea scallops
1 tablespoon margarine
8 ounces mushrooms, sliced
2 tablespoons sherry
2 tablespoons flour
⅛ teaspoon pepper
1 cup fat-free sour cream

Dissolve the bouillon cube in the hot water and mix well. Rinse the shrimp and scallops and pat dry. Heat the margarine in a large skillet until melted. Add the shrimp and scallops. Cook for 5 minutes or until the shrimp turn pink and the scallops are tender, stirring frequently. Remove the shrimp and scallops with a slotted spoon to a bowl, reserving the pan drippings. Stir the mushrooms and sherry into the reserved pan drippings. Cook until the mushrooms are tender, stirring frequently. Stir in a mixture of the bouillon, flour and pepper. Cook until the sauce comes to a boil and thickens slightly, stirring constantly; reduce heat. Stir in the sour cream. Add the shrimp and scallops. Cook just until heated through, stirring frequently. Serve over hot cooked wild rice. **Yield:** 6 servings.

Per Serving:
Calories: 218; Carbohydrate: 13 g; Protein: 31 g; Total Fat: 4 g;
Cholesterol: 146 mg; Sodium: 298 mg; Fiber: trace;
Calories from Fat: 17%

Black Beans and Rice

1 onion, chopped ♦ 1 red pepper, chopped
1 tablespoon garlic powder ♦ 3 tablespoons olive oil
4 (16-ounce) cans black beans, drained, rinsed
2 pouches boil-in-bag rice, cooked

Sauté the onion, red pepper and garlic powder in the olive oil in a saucepan. Stir in the beans. Cook for 5 minutes or until heated through, stirring occasionally. Serve over the rice. **Yield:** 8 servings.

Per Serving:
Calories: 375; Carbohydrate: 64 g; Protein: 17.5 g; Total Fat: 6 g;
Cholesterol: 0 mg; Sodium: 227 mg; Fiber: 7.5 g;
Calories from Fat: 14%

Red Beans and Rice

12 ounces dried red beans ♦ 6 cups low-sodium chicken broth
2 cups finely chopped onion ♦ 2 cups finely chopped celery
1 cup finely chopped green bell pepper
1½ tablespoons finely minced garlic
1 tablespoon finely julienned sun-dried tomato
1 bay leaf ♦ ½ teaspoon thyme ♦ ½ teaspoon white pepper
¼ teaspoon salt ♦ ¼ teaspoon cayenne ♦ 2 cups rice

Sort and rinse the red beans. Combine the red beans with enough water to cover in a bowl. Let stand for 8 to 10 hours. Drain and rinse. Mix the red beans and the next 11 ingredients in a stockpot. Bring to a boil; reduce heat. Simmer, covered, for 1½ to 1¾ hours or until the beans are tender, stirring occasionally. Stir in the rice. Cook for 25 minutes longer or until the rice is tender, stirring occasionally. Discard the bay leaf. Adjust the seasonings. **Yield:** 12 servings.

Per Serving:
Calories: 206; Carbohydrate: 40 g; Protein: 9 g; Total Fat: 0.6 g;
Cholesterol: 0 mg; Sodium: 87 mg; Fiber: trace;
Calories from Fat: 3%

On the Go

Lasagna with Bean Sauce

1 tablespoon olive oil
1 small onion, minced
2 teaspoons minced garlic
2 cups coarsely chopped drained cooked pinto beans
2 cups no-salt-added tomato sauce
2 cups no-salt-added tomato purée
1 teaspoon oregano
1 teaspoon basil
Pepper to taste
12 ounces uncooked lasagna noodles
2 cups part-skim ricotta cheese
8 ounces part-skim mozzarella cheese, sliced
¼ cup grated fat-free Parmesan cheese

Heat the olive oil in a large skillet. Add the onion and garlic. Sauté until tender. Stir in the beans. Cook for 2 to 3 minutes, stirring constantly. Add the tomato sauce, tomato purée, oregano, basil and pepper. Bring to a boil; reduce heat. Simmer for 5 minutes, stirring occasionally. Spread a thin layer of the sauce in a 9x13-inch baking dish. Layer ⅓ of the noodles, ½ of the ricotta cheese, ½ of the mozzarella cheese and ⅓ of the remaining sauce in the prepared dish. Continue layering with half the remaining noodles, half the remaining sauce, remaining ricotta cheese, remaining mozzarella cheese, remaining noodles and remaining sauce. Sprinkle with the Parmesan cheese. Bake, covered, at 350 degrees for 1 hour.
Yield: 12 servings.

Per Serving:
Calories: 299; Carbohydrate: 38 g; Protein: 17 g; Total Fat: 8.7 g;
Cholesterol: 24.6 mg; Sodium: 338 mg; Fiber: 2.4 g;
Calories from Fat: 26%

Rainbow Fruit Dessert Pizza

3½ cups miniature marshmallows, or 35 regular marshmallows
1 tablespoon melted margarine
5 cups cornflakes or crisp rice cereal
8 ounces nonfat cream cheese
¼ cup fruit preserves
1 teaspoon vanilla extract
4 cups assorted chopped or sliced fresh fruit
¼ cup fruit preserves
2 tablespoons water

Spray a pizza pan or 2 pie plates with nonstick cooking spray. Combine the marshmallows and margarine in a large microwave-safe bowl. Microwave on High for 1½ to 2 minutes or until the marshmallows melt, stirring at 1 minute intervals. Add the cereal, stirring until coated. Press the cereal mixture into the prepared pizza pan or pie plates with moistened fingers. Beat the cream cheese, ¼ cup fruit preserves and vanilla in a mixer bowl until well mixed. Spread over the prepared layer. Arrange the fruit in a decorative pattern over the top. Combine ¼ cup fruit preserves and water in a bowl and mix well. Drizzle over the fruit. **Yield:** 16 servings.

Per Serving:
Calories: 160; Carbohydrate: 28 g; Protein: 2 g; Total Fat: 1 g;
Cholesterol: 3 mg; Sodium: 297 mg; Fiber: trace;
Calories from Fat: 5%

To save money grocery shopping, comparison shop and use coupons. Buy store brands or no-frills to economize on heart-smart foods.

On the Go

BEYOND OAT BRAN

Remember the days when an older gentleman with a walrus-like mustache appeared on television commercials, telling us that we should eat oats "because they're good for you"? And like lemmings heading for the edge of the cliff, we hurried to add oat bran to our diets, convinced it was the new, magic thing that would make us healthier and help us to lose weight the easy way. Unfortunately, the paid commercial spokesperson failed to mention that many of us would come to think that oat bran tastes like sawdust.

One positive result of this campaign was that it challenged us to think about what we eat for breakfast. Even today, we're surrounded by "all-you-can-eat" breakfast bars and breakfast specials that offer lumberjack-sized portions of eggs, pork breakfast meats, gravy, biscuits, and grits. We've come to realize that even though we think it's a treat to have a "country-style" breakfast, the gigantic American farm breakfast is no longer practical because few of us are going to work in the fields when we push back from the breakfast table. Eggs and bacon and biscuits and gravy are not only high in fat and cholesterol, they simply add up to too much food, and that means unwanted weight gain. Hence, we offer some alternative choices to begin your day. You can bring home the bacon; just eat it sparingly!

1890's photograph of a mother and her son. Inset: Belle Meade Mansion, built in 1853, is today a historical landmark and open to the public.

Quiche Lorraine Then

¼ cup butter
4 small onions, chopped
1 teaspoon salt
6 slices bacon
1 cup grated Gruyère
cheese
2 egg yolks
2 whole eggs
1½ cups light cream

Per Serving:
Calories: 320;
Carbohydrate: 3 g;
Protein: 9 g;
Total Fat: 25 g;
Cholesterol: 203 mg;
Sodium: 510 mg;
Fiber: trace;
Calories from Fat: 70%

Beyond Oat Bran

No-Crust Quiche Now

2 cups skim milk
1 cup egg substitute
1 cup shredded fat-free Cheddar cheese
1 cup chopped assorted vegetables
¼ teaspoon salt
¼ teaspoon sugar
⅛ teaspoon cayenne

Combine the skim milk, egg substitute, cheese, vegetables, salt, sugar and cayenne in a bowl and mix well. Pour into a pie plate sprayed with nonstick cooking spray. Bake at 325 degrees for 15 to 20 minutes or until set. May microwave until knife inserted in center comes out clean. **Yield:** 6 servings.

Per Serving:
Calories: 80; Carbohydrate: 6.9 g; Protein: 12.5 g; Total Fat: 0.1 g;
Cholesterol: 3 mg; Sodium: 305 mg; Fiber: trace;
Calories from Fat: 1%

Banana Split Smoothies

1¼ cups sliced ripe bananas
1 (8-ounce) can juice-pack crushed pineapple
1 cup crushed ice
½ cup unsweetened orange juice
1 teaspoon sugar
1 cup vanilla low-fat yogurt

Combine the bananas, undrained pineapple, ice, orange juice and sugar in a blender container. Process until smooth. Add the yogurt. Process until blended. Serve immediately.
Yield: 4 (1-cup) servings.

Per Serving:
Calories: 138; Carbohydrate: 30.7 g; Protein: 3.79 g; Total Fat: 1 g;
Cholesterol: 3 mg; Sodium: 39 mg; Fiber: trace;
Calories from Fat: 7%

Vegetable and Cheddar Cheese Omelet

½ cup egg substitute
1 ounce shredded fat-free Cheddar cheese
½ cup chopped assorted raw vegetables
(such as green pepper, onion, mushrooms, broccoli)

Spray a skillet with nonstick cooking spray. Heat the skillet over medium-high heat until hot. Pour the egg substitute into the prepared skillet. Cook until almost set; turn the omelet. Sprinkle with the cheese and vegetables; fold in half. Cook until the cheese melts. Serve immediately. **Yield:** 1 (1-omelet) serving.

Per Serving:
Calories: 112; Carbohydrate: 6.5 g; Protein: 20 g; Total Fat: 0 g;
Cholesterol: <5 mg; Sodium: 350 mg; Fiber: trace;
Calories from Fat: 0%

Beyond Oat Bran

For ground rolled oats, process in a blender or food processor.

APRICOT NUT BREAD

2½ cups flour ♦ 1 cup sugar
1½ tablespoons baking powder ♦ ½ teaspoon (or less) light salt
½ cup apple or peach butter ♦ ½ cup skim milk
¼ cup orange juice ♦ 2 egg whites ♦ 4 teaspoons grated orange peel
10 large dried apricot halves, chopped ♦ ¼ cup chopped pecans

Mix the first 4 ingredients in a mixer bowl. Add the next 5 ingredients. Beat at medium speed for 30 seconds or just until blended. Fold in the apricots and pecans. Spoon into an oiled and floured 5x9-inch loaf pan. Bake at 350 degrees for 35 to 45 minutes or until the loaf tests done. Cool in the pan for 5 minutes. Invert onto wire rack to cool completely. **Yield:** 10 (1-slice) servings.

PER SERVING:
CALORIES: 233; CARBOHYDRATE: 48 g; PROTEIN: 46 g; TOTAL FAT: 2 g;
CHOLESTEROL: trace; SODIUM: 128 mg; FIBER: trace;
CALORIES FROM FAT: 9%

OATMEAL BISCUITS

¼ cup rolled oats, ground ♦ ½ cup flour ♦ 1 teaspoon brown sugar
¾ teaspoon baking powder ♦ ¼ teaspoon baking soda
Salt to taste ♦ 1½ tablespoons reduced-calorie margarine
⅓ cup low-fat buttermilk ♦ 2 teaspoons flour

Mix the first 6 ingredients in a bowl. Cut in the margarine until crumbly. Add the buttermilk, stirring until moistened. Sprinkle 2 teaspoons flour over the work surface. Knead 10 to 12 times. Roll ½ inch thick; cut with a 2-inch cutter. Arrange the biscuits on a baking sheet coated with nonstick cooking spray. Bake at 400 degrees for 10 minutes or until light brown. **Yield:** 4 (1-biscuit) servings.

PER SERVING:
CALORIES: 111; CARBOHYDRATE: 17 g; PROTEIN: 3 g; TOTAL FAT: 4 g;
CHOLESTEROL: 0 mg; SODIUM: 208 mg; FIBER: 1 g;
CALORIES FROM FAT: 28%

Easy Orange Spice Biscuits

3½ cups reduced-fat baking mix
3 tablespoons sugar
3 tablespoons orange instant breakfast drink mix
2½ teaspoons cinnamon
1¼ cups skim milk
1½ cups confectioners' sugar
2 tablespoons orange juice
¼ teaspoon vanilla extract

Combine the baking mix, sugar, drink mix and cinnamon in a bowl and mix well. Add the skim milk, stirring just until moistened. Drop by rounded tablespoonfuls onto a baking sheet sprayed with nonstick cooking spray. Bake at 425 degrees for 10 minutes or until golden brown. Combine the confectioners' sugar, orange juice and vanilla in a bowl, stirring until of glaze consistency. Drizzle over the hot biscuits. Serve immediately. **Yield:** 22 (1-biscuit) servings.

Per Serving:
Calories: 119; Carbohydrate: 25 g; Protein: 2 g; Total Fat: 1 g;
Cholesterol: trace; Sodium: 227 mg; Fiber: trace;
Calories from Fat: 9%

Small amounts of sodium are used by the body to uphold and regulate the correct water balance. Excess sodium is thought to contribute to water retention, high blood pressure, and kidney disease.

Beyond Oat Bran

HARVEST APPLE COFFEE CAKE

2 cups all-purpose flour
1 cup whole wheat flour
1 cup sugar
1½ teaspoons cinnamon
1 teaspoon baking powder
6 egg whites
½ cup sugar
1 cup unsweetened applesauce
1 teaspoon vanilla extract
3 medium apples (1 pound), peeled, finely chopped
1 cup raisins
½ cup chopped walnuts
Confectioners' sugar to taste (optional)

Spray a 10-inch nonstick tube pan with nonstick cooking spray. Combine the all-purpose flour, whole wheat flour, 1 cup sugar, cinnamon and baking powder in a bowl and mix well. Beat the egg whites in a mixer bowl until soft peaks form. Beat in ½ cup sugar gradually at low speed. Add the applesauce and vanilla gradually, beating at low speed until blended. Beat in ¼ of the flour mixture gradually, mixing well after each addition. Fold into the remaining flour mixture. Fold in the apples, raisins and walnuts. Spoon into the prepared tube pan. Bake at 350 degrees for 1 hour or until a wooden pick inserted near the center comes out clean. Cool in the pan on a wire rack for 10 minutes. Invert onto a serving platter. Cool slightly. Dust the top lightly with confectioners' sugar. Serve warm.
Yield: 12 servings.

PER SERVING:
CALORIES: 321; CARBOHYDRATE: 69 g; PROTEIN: 6 g; TOTAL FAT: 3 g;
CHOLESTEROL: 0 mg; SODIUM: 64 mg; FIBER: trace;
CALORIES FROM FAT: 10%

Low-Fat Morning Glory Muffins

2¼ cups flour
1¼ cups sugar
1 tablespoon cinnamon
2 teaspoons baking soda
⅛ teaspoon salt
2 cups grated carrots
1 apple, shredded
½ cup raisins
1 (8-ounce) can juice-pack crushed pineapple, drained
½ cup egg substitute
1 egg white
⅓ cup applesauce
¼ cup low-fat buttermilk
¼ cup canola oil
1 teaspoon ground cloves
1 teaspoon vanilla extract

Grease 16 muffin cups or line muffin cups with paper liners. Sift the flour, sugar, cinnamon, baking soda and salt into a bowl and mix well. Stir in the carrots, apple, raisins and pineapple. Whisk the egg substitute, egg white, applesauce, buttermilk, canola oil, cloves and vanilla in a bowl. Add to the flour mixture, stirring just until moistened. Fill the prepared muffin cups ¾ full. Bake at 350 degrees for 35 minutes or until a wooden pick inserted in the center comes out clean. Cool the muffins in the pans for 10 minutes. Invert onto a wire rack to cool completely. Store in an airtight container.
Yield: 16 (1-muffin) servings.

Per Serving:
Calories: 204; Carbohydrate: 40 g; Protein: 3 g; Total Fat: 4 g;
Cholesterol: trace; Sodium: 160 mg; Fiber: trace;
Calories from Fat: 17%

Beyond Oat Bran

Cinnamon Orange Pancakes

¾ cup all-purpose flour ♦ 1 cup whole wheat flour
2 tablespoons wheat germ ♦ 1 tablespoon sugar
2 teaspoons baking powder ♦ 1 teaspoon cinnamon
1 cup skim milk ♦ ¾ cup fresh orange juice
Egg substitute equivalent to 1 egg ♦ 1 teaspoon grated orange peel

Combine the first 6 ingredients in a bowl and mix well. Combine the skim milk, orange juice, egg substitute and orange peel in a bowl and mix well. Add to the dry ingredients, stirring just until moistened. Spray a hot griddle or nonstick skillet with nonstick cooking spray. Pour ¼ cup batter for each pancake onto the griddle. Bake until bubbles appear on top and the edges are dry; turn. Bake until brown. **Yield:** 6 (2-pancake) servings.

PER SERVING:
CALORIES: 171; CARBOHYDRATE: 34 g; PROTEIN: 7 g; TOTAL FAT: 1 g;
CHOLESTEROL: 1 mg; SODIUM: 140 mg; FIBER: trace;
CALORIES FROM FAT: 5%

Cholesterol-Free Popovers

6 egg whites ♦ 1 cup skim milk ♦ 2 tablespoons melted margarine
1 cup bread flour or all-purpose flour ♦ ¼ teaspoon salt

Spray the muffin cups with nonstick cooking spray. Beat the egg whites in a mixer bowl at high speed until foamy. Add the skim milk and margarine. Beat at medium speed until blended. Add the bread flour and salt gradually, beating constantly until smooth. Fill the prepared muffin cups ¾ full. Bake at 375 degrees for 45 minutes. Cut a small slit in the top of each popover. Bake for 5 minutes longer. Serve immediately. **Yield:** 12 (1-popover) servings.

PER SERVING:
CALORIES: 69; CARBOHYDRATE: 8 g; PROTEIN: 4 g; TOTAL FAT: 2 g;
CHOLESTEROL: 0 mg; SODIUM: 109 mg; FIBER: trace;
CALORIES FROM FAT: 30%

Belgian Waffles

2 cups flour
1 tablespoon plus 1 teaspoon baking powder
1 tablespoon sugar
¼ teaspoon salt
1½ cups skim milk
½ cup frozen egg substitute, thawed
¼ cup melted reduced-calorie margarine
½ teaspoon vanilla extract
2 tablespoons confectioners' sugar
Sliced strawberries (optional)
Fresh mint sprigs (optional)

Combine the flour, baking powder, sugar and salt in a mixer bowl and mix well. Combine the skim milk, egg substitute, margarine and vanilla in a bowl and mix well. Add to the dry ingredients. Beat at medium speed until blended. Spray a Belgian waffle iron with nonstick cooking spray; heat. Spoon ¼ cup batter onto the hot waffle iron, spreading the batter to edges. Bake for 4 to 5 minutes or until the steam stops. Repeat the process with the remaining batter. Sprinkle the confectioners' sugar over the waffles. Top with strawberries and mint sprigs. **Yield:** 12 (4-inch waffle) servings.

Per Serving:
Calories: 118; Carbohydrate: 19 g; Protein: 4 g; Total Fat: 3 g;
Cholesterol: 1 mg; Sodium: 217 mg; Fiber: 1 g;
Calories from Fat: 22%

If you visit high elevation areas, be cautious with your exercise effort. Slow down, walk for a shorter period of time, and drink plenty of fluids.

Beyond Oat Bran

Monounsaturated fats are "good fats." When combined with exercise they may help increase good cholesterol or HDL. Examples of monounsaturated fats include canola, olive, and peanut oils.

APRICOT CREAM CHEESE SPREAD

8 ounces nonfat cream cheese, softened
⅓ cup All-Fruit apricot preserves, or to taste

Combine the cream cheese and preserves in a bowl, mixing until of the desired consistency and flavor. Spread on bagels, toast, English muffins or the bread of your choice.
Yield: 16 (1-tablespoon) servings.

PER SERVING:
CALORIES: 31; CARBOHYDRATE: 2 g; PROTEIN: 2 g; TOTAL FAT: 0 g;
CHOLESTEROL: <2.5 mg; SODIUM: 91 mg; FIBER: trace;
CALORIES FROM FAT: 0%

BLACKBERRY SPREAD

3 cups fresh blackberries
¼ cup sugar
1 (1¾-ounce) envelope powdered pectin
1 tablespoon unsweetened orange juice

Crush the blackberries in a bowl. Combine the blackberries with juice, sugar, pectin and orange juice in a saucepan and mix well. Bring to a boil. Boil for 1 minute, stirring constantly. Remove from heat. Stir for 3 minutes. Pour into freezer containers immediately, leaving ½-inch headspace; cover with lids. Let stand until room temperature. Freeze. Thaw before serving.
Yield: 32 (1-tablespoon) servings.

PER SERVING:
CALORIES: 18; CARBOHYDRATE: 5 g; PROTEIN: 0 g; TOTAL FAT: 0 g;
CHOLESTEROL: 0 mg; SODIUM: 0 mg; FIBER: 1 g;
CALORIES FROM FAT: 0%

Blueberry Syrup

¼ cup sugar
1½ tablespoons cornstarch
1 cup boiling water
1 (16-ounce) package frozen unsweetened blueberries,
thawed, drained
1 tablespoon lemon juice

Combine the sugar and cornstarch in a saucepan and mix well. Stir in the boiling water gradually. Bring to a boil over medium heat, stirring constantly; reduce heat. Simmer for 1 minute, stirring constantly. Remove from heat. Stir in the blueberries and lemon juice. Serve warm or chilled over pancakes or waffles.
Yield: 32 (1-tablespoon) servings.

Per Serving:
Calories: 15; Carbohydrate: 4 g; Protein: 0 g; Total Fat: trace;
Cholesterol: 0 mg; Sodium: 0 mg; Fiber: 1 g;
Calories from Fat: 6%

Maple and Apple Butter Syrup

6 ounces apple butter
4 ounces unfiltered fresh apple cider
6 ounces maple syrup

Combine the apple butter and apple cider in a saucepan and mix well. Bring to a simmer, stirring frequently. Stir in the maple syrup. Bring to a simmer, stirring frequently. Serve warm or chilled over pancakes or waffles. **Yield:** 16 (2-tablespoon) servings.

Per Serving:
Calories: 55; Carbohydrate: 13 g; Protein: trace; Total Fat: trace;
Cholesterol: 0 mg; Sodium: 5 mg; Fiber: trace;
Calories from Fat: 0%

Beyond Oat Bran

Believe it or not, there *was* a time when daily meals were considered incomplete without a dessert. Many households served a different dessert nightly at the dinner table, and often at the midday meal as well.

All the pies, cakes, cookies, cobblers, and other sugar-laden confections helped pile on the calories and fat, leading to adults with ever-expanding waistlines. Of course, in those days, the career homemaker's apron could hide the matronly bulges, and men's bodies certainly were not appraised as directly by mates or dates.

Nowadays, celebrity bodies are displayed everywhere: advertisements, television, the movies. Physical perfection—or at least, an attempt at looking more fit—is unattainable without making changes in our daily habits.

It is possible to enjoy saintly desserts without committing unforgivable dietary "sins". Dietary diehards seem to take an "all-or-nothing-at-all" approach about desserts, but a few modifications here and there can make a big difference in the impact this one component of our eating habits has on our overall fitness.

So don't throw away Mama's best cake recipe; just pick one of our desserts the next time you're planning something special.

Union Station, built in 1900 by the Louisville and Nashville Railroad (L&N) and the Nashville, Chattanooga and St. Louis (N.C. & St. L.) Railroad Companies. Inset: 1996, the refurbished lobby of the Union Station Hotel.

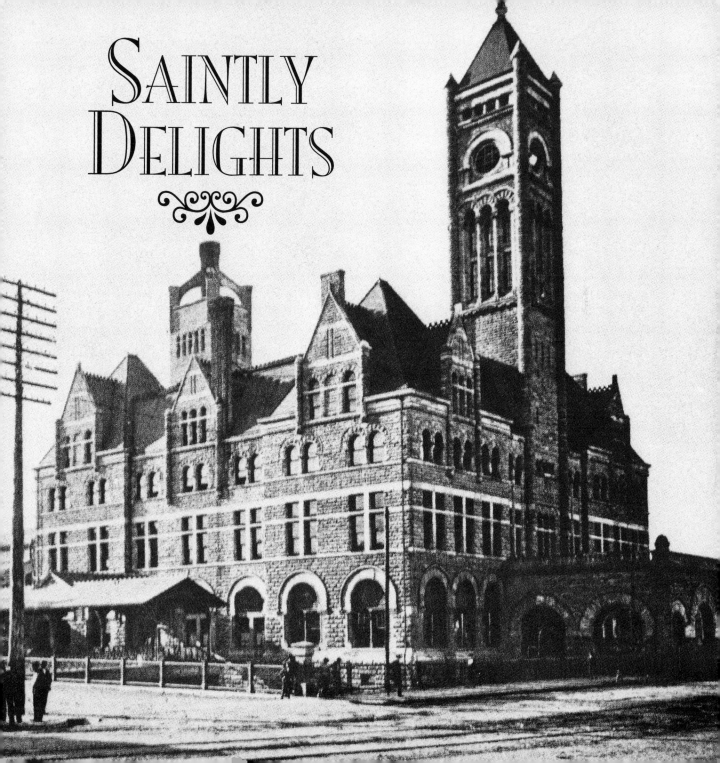

SAINTLY
DELIGHTS

Carrot Cake Then

4 eggs
1½ cups vegetable oil
2 cups flour
2 cups sugar
1 tablespoon cinnamon
2 teaspoons baking
powder
2 teaspoons baking soda
1 teaspoon salt
3 cups grated carrots
1 cup chopped black
walnuts
1 (1-pound) package
confectioners' sugar
½ cup butter
8 ounces cream cheese

Per Serving:
Calories: 585;
Carbohydrate: 83 g;
Protein: 9 g; Total Fat: 50 g;
Cholesterol: 135 mg;
Sodium: 622 mg; Fiber: trace;
Calories from Fat: 77%

Saintly Delights

Carrot Cake Now

1½ cups unbleached flour ♦ ¼ cup wheat germ
2 teaspoons baking soda ♦ 2 teaspoons baking powder
2 teaspoons cinnamon ♦ ¼ teaspoon salt
1 cup packed brown sugar ♦ 1 cup egg substitute
1 cup plain nonfat yogurt ♦ 1 teaspoon vanilla extract
1 cup raisins
1 (8-ounce) can juice-pack crushed pineapple, drained
2 cups shredded carrots ♦ 4 ounces light cream cheese, softened
1½ cups confectioners' sugar ♦ 2 teaspoons lemon juice
1 teaspoon vanilla extract

Combine the flour, wheat germ, baking soda, baking powder, cinnamon and salt in a bowl and mix well. Beat the brown sugar, egg substitute, yogurt and 1 teaspoon vanilla in a mixer bowl until blended. Add the flour mixture gradually, beating just until moistened; scrape the side of the bowl occasionally. Dust the raisins with additional flour. Fold the raisins, pineapple and carrots into the batter. Spoon into a 9x13-inch cake pan sprayed with nonstick cooking spray. Bake at 350 degrees for 30 to 40 minutes or until the cake tests done. Cool in the pan on a wire rack. Beat the cream cheese in a mixer bowl until creamy. Add the confectioners' sugar gradually, beating constantly at low speed until fluffy. Add the lemon juice and 1 teaspoon vanilla. Beat until of spreading consistency. Spread over the cake. **Yield:** 16 servings.

Per Serving:
Calories: 258; Carbohydrate: 47 g; Protein: 5 g; Total Fat: 2 g;
Cholesterol: 7 mg; Sodium: 258 mg; Fiber: trace;
Calories from Fat: 7%

Apple Crisp

6 or 7 tart apples, peeled, sliced ♦ 1 tablespoon lemon juice
⅓ cup sugar ♦ 1 teaspoon cinnamon ♦ ½ cup raisins
1 cup packed brown sugar ♦ ¾ cup rolled oats ♦ ½ cup flour

Place the apples in a deep baking dish sprayed with nonstick cooking spray. Sprinkle with the lemon juice, sugar, cinnamon and raisins. Spray with butter-flavor nonstick cooking spray. Sprinkle mixture of remaining ingredients over the top. Spray with fat-free spray margarine. Bake at 375 degrees for 30 minutes.
Yield: 12 servings.

PER SERVING:
CALORIES: 183; CARBOHYDRATE: 45 g; PROTEIN: 1.7 g; TOTAL FAT: 0.6 g;
CHOLESTEROL: 0 mg; SODIUM: 8 mg; FIBER: 2.2 g;
CALORIES FROM FAT: 3%

Sugar-Free Peach Cobbler

1 (6-ounce) can frozen apple juice concentrate
½ apple juice can water ♦ 2 tablespoons cornstarch
1 teaspoon cinnamon
1 (20-ounce) package frozen no-sugar-added peaches
1 cup flour ♦ 3 tablespoons vegetable oil
3 tablespoons water ♦ Salt to taste

Mix the first 4 ingredients in a saucepan. Cook over medium heat until thickened. Stir in the peaches. Spoon into an 8x8-inch baking dish. Mix the remaining ingredients in a bowl until the dough pulls from the side of the bowl. Roll between sheets of waxed paper. Place the dough over top of peaches; prick with a fork. Bake at 375 degrees for 40 to 45 minutes or until brown. **Yield:** 8 servings.

PER SERVING:
CALORIES: 183; CARBOHYDRATE: 32 g; PROTEIN: 2.2 g; TOTAL FAT: 5.3 g;
CHOLESTEROL: 0 mg; SODIUM: 43.8 mg; FIBER: 0.3 g;
CALORIES FROM FAT: 26%

ALMOND POUND CAKE

2½ cups flour ◆ 1 cup sugar ◆ ½ teaspoon salt
½ teaspoon baking soda ◆ 1 cup plain nonfat yogurt
½ cup egg substitute ◆ ¼ cup low-fat buttermilk
¼ cup canola oil ◆ 2 teaspoons almond extract
1 teaspoon vanilla extract

Mix the flour, sugar, salt and baking soda in a mixer bowl. Add the yogurt, egg substitute, buttermilk, canola oil and flavorings. Beat at medium to high speed for 3 minutes, scraping the bowl occasionally. Spoon into a 10-inch nonstick bundt pan sprayed with nonstick cooking spray. Bake at 350 degrees for 60 to 70 minutes or until the cake tests done. Cool in pan for 15 minutes. Invert onto wire rack to cool completely. Cut into 1-inch slices. **Yield:** 20 servings.

PER SERVING:
CALORIES: 133; CARBOHYDRATE: 23.3 g; PROTEIN: 2.9 g; TOTAL FAT: 3.1 g;
CHOLESTEROL: trace; SODIUM: 97 mg; FIBER: trace;
CALORIES FROM FAT: 21%

DEVIL'S FOOD POUND CAKE

1 (2-layer) package devil's food cake mix
1 package sugar-free fat-free chocolate instant pudding mix
1¼ cups water ◆ ½ cup applesauce ◆ 8 ounces egg substitute

Grease and flour a cake pan. Combine all the ingredients in a mixer bowl and blend well. Beat at medium speed for 2 minutes, scraping bowl occasionally. Bake at 350 degrees for 50 to 60 minutes or until wooden pick inserted in center comes out clean. Cool in pan for 25 minutes. Invert onto a wire rack to cool completely. Bake at 325 degrees if using a heavy coated bundt pan. **Yield:** 16 servings.

PER SERVING:
CALORIES: 158; CARBOHYDRATE: 29.3 g; PROTEIN: 3.1 g; TOTAL FAT: 3 g;
CHOLESTEROL: 0 mg; SODIUM: 373 mg; FIBER: trace;
CALORIES FROM FAT: 17%

Strawberry Shortcake

1 pint strawberries, sliced
2 tablespoons sugar
1 tablespoon water
1¼ cups flour
2 tablespoons sugar
1½ teaspoons baking powder
¼ teaspoon salt
2 tablespoons reduced-calorie margarine
¼ cup egg substitute
3 tablespoons unsweetened applesauce
2 tablespoons skim milk
1 teaspoon finely shredded lemon peel (optional)

Place the strawberries in a bowl. Sprinkle with 2 tablespoons sugar, tossing lightly. Sprinkle with the water. Combine the flour, 2 tablespoons sugar, baking powder and salt in a bowl and mix well. Cut in the margarine until crumbly. Add the egg substitute, applesauce, skim milk and lemon peel, stirring just until moistened; do not overmix. Divide the dough into 4 equal portions. Shape each portion into a ball. Roll each dough ball into a circle ½ inch thick on a lightly floured surface. Place on a lightly greased baking sheet. Bake at 450 degrees for 8 to 10 minutes or until golden brown. Remove to a wire rack to cool. Split each shortcake horizontally into halves. Place the bottom half of each shortcake on each of 4 dessert plates. Layer the bottoms with ½ of the strawberries, the remaining shortcake tops and the remaining strawberries. Serve with frozen vanilla nonfat or low-fat yogurt if desired. **Yield:** 4 servings.

Per Serving:
Calories: 221; Carbohydrate: 51 g; Protein: 6 g; Total Fat: 5 g;
Cholesterol: 0 mg; Sodium: 363 mg; Fiber: 3 g;
Calories from Fat: 22%

In recipes for baked goods, the sugar can often be reduced by ¼ to ⅓ without harm to the final product. Cinnamon and vanilla extract also give a sweet impression.

Saintly Delights

Date Bars

¾ cup sugar ♦ 1 egg
2 egg whites
1 cup flour ♦ 1 teaspoon baking powder
1½ cups sliced dates
¼ cup pecan pieces
1 teaspoon vanilla extract

Beat the sugar, egg and egg whites in a mixer bowl until thickened, scraping the bowl occasionally. Add the flour and baking powder. Beat until smooth. Fold in the dates, pecans and vanilla. Spoon into a 9x13-inch baking dish lined with waxed paper. Bake at 350 degrees for 30 minutes. Cut into 1x4-inch bars while warm. May roll in confectioners' sugar. **Yield:** 24 bars.

Per Serving:
Calories: 192; Carbohydrate: 37 g; Protein: 3 g; Total Fat: 3.7 g;
Cholesterol: 18 mg; Sodium: 50 mg; Fiber: 2.7 g;
Calories from Fat: 17%

Low-Fat Cheesecake

12 ounces nonfat cream cheese, softened
¾ cup sugar ♦ 4 egg whites
1 tablespoon pure lemon juice
1 (9-inch) graham cracker pie shell

Beat the cream cheese and sugar in a mixer bowl until creamy. Add the egg whites and lemon juice. Beat until light and fluffy, scraping the bowl occasionally. Spoon into the pie shell. Bake at 350 degrees for 35 minutes or until light brown. Let stand until cool. **Yield:** 10 servings.

Per Serving:
Calories: 195; Carbohydrate: 32 g; Protein: 7.6 g; Total Fat: 4.3 g;
Cholesterol: 4 mg; Sodium: 301 mg; Fiber: trace;
Calories from Fat: 23%

Chocolate Amaretto Cheesecake

6 chocolate wafers, finely crushed
1½ cups nonfat cream cheese
1 cup sugar
1 cup 1% cottage cheese, drained in cheesecloth
¼ cup plus 2 tablespoons baking cocoa
¼ cup flour
¼ cup amaretto
1 teaspoon vanilla extract
¼ teaspoon salt
1 egg
2 tablespoons miniature semisweet chocolate chips

Sprinkle the wafer crumbs evenly over the bottom of a 7-inch springform pan. Combine the cream cheese, sugar, cottage cheese, baking cocoa, flour, amaretto, vanilla and salt in a food processor container fitted with a steel blade. Process until smooth. Add the egg. Process just until blended. Fold in the chocolate chips. Spoon over the prepared layer. Bake at 300 degrees for 65 to 70 minutes or until set. Cool in the pan on a wire rack. Chill, covered, for 8 hours or longer. Remove the side of the springform pan; transfer the cheesecake to a serving platter. Garnish with fresh raspberries and confectioners' sugar. Decrease the baking time to 45 to 50 minutes if using an 8-inch springform pan. **Yield:** 12 servings.

Per Serving:
Calories: 155; Carbohydrate: 27.2 g; Protein: 6.7 g; Total Fat: 2.9 g;
Cholesterol: 26.1 mg; Sodium: 293 mg; Fiber: trace;
Calories from Fat: 17%

Instead of ice cream, choose sherbet, sorbet, 1 percent ice milk, frozen low-fat yogurt, or pudding made with skim milk.

Saintly Delights

Lemon Cheesecake

2 tablespoons graham cracker crumbs
1 (10½-ounce) package soft tofu, drained
8 ounces nonfat cream cheese
1 cup 1% cottage cheese
½ cup sugar
¼ cup honey
2 tablespoons lemon juice
1 teaspoon grated lemon peel
1 teaspoon lemon extract
1 teaspoon vanilla extract
1 egg
2 egg whites
1 cup sliced fresh strawberries
2 small lemons, thinly sliced

Spray a 9-inch springform pan with nonstick cooking spray. Sprinkle the graham cracker crumbs over the bottom and side of the prepared pan. Combine the tofu, cream cheese, cottage cheese, sugar, honey, lemon juice, lemon peel and flavorings in a blender or food processor container. Process until smooth. Add the egg and egg whites 1 at a time, processing just until blended after each addition. Spoon into the prepared pan. Bake at 300 degrees for 1 hour. Turn off the oven. Let stand in oven with door closed for 1 hour. Chill, covered, in the refrigerator. Remove the side of the pan. Transfer to a serving platter. Top with the strawberries and lemon slices.
Yield: 12 servings.

Per Serving:
Calories: 120; Carbohydrate: 20 g; Protein: 7.0 g; Total Fat: 1.3 g;
Cholesterol: 20.6 mg; Sodium: 204 mg; Fiber: trace;
Calories from Fat: 10%

Pumpkin Cheesecake

1 cup graham cracker crumbs
1 (16-ounce) can pumpkin
12 ounces nonfat cream cheese
1 cup fat-free ricotta cheese
½ cup packed dark brown sugar
1 tablespoon melted margarine
1 tablespoon plus 1½ teaspoons flour
1½ teaspoons vanilla extract
1½ teaspoons pumpkin pie spice
1 teaspoon brandy flavoring
½ cup egg substitute

Spray a 9-inch springform pan with nonstick cooking spray. Sprinkle the graham cracker crumbs over the bottom and side of the prepared pan. Combine the pumpkin, cream cheese, ricotta cheese, brown sugar, margarine, flour, vanilla, pumpkin pie spice and brandy flavoring in a blender or food processor container. Process until smooth. Add the egg substitute ¼ cup at a time, processing after each addition just until blended. Spoon into the prepared pan. Place the springform pan in a large shallow baking pan. Pour hot water to a depth of 1 inch into the larger pan. Bake at 350 degrees for 50 minutes or until almost set. Turn off oven. Let stand in oven with door slightly ajar for 30 minutes. Remove the springform pan to a wire rack to cool. Chill, covered, in the refrigerator. Remove the side of the pan. Transfer the cheesecake to a serving platter.
Yield: 12 servings.

Per Serving:
Calories: 154; Carbohydrate: 24 g; Protein: 8.8 g; Total Fat: 2.1 g;
Cholesterol: 9.6 mg; Sodium: 227 mg; Fiber: trace;
Calories from Fat: 12%

Select fat-reduced and fat-free desserts, pastries, and baked goods whenever possible. A low-fat product should contain 2 grams of fat or less per serving.

Saintly Delights

LEMON MERINGUE PIE

⅔ cup sugar
⅓ cup cornstarch
2 cups skim milk
½ cup frozen egg substitute, thawed
⅓ cup fresh lemon juice
2 teaspoons grated lemon peel
1 baked (9-inch) Low-Fat Pie Crust (page 138)
4 egg whites
½ teaspoon cream of tartar
½ teaspoon vanilla extract
2 tablespoons sugar

Combine ⅔ cup sugar and cornstarch in a saucepan and mix well. Stir in the skim milk gradually. Bring to a boil over medium heat, stirring constantly. Boil for 1 minute. Remove from heat. Stir ¼ of the hot mixture gradually into the egg substitute. Stir the egg substitute into the hot mixture. Cook over medium heat for 2 minutes, stirring constantly. Remove from heat. Stir in the lemon juice and lemon peel. Spoon into the crust. Beat the egg whites, cream of tartar and vanilla in a mixer bowl at high speed until foamy. Add 2 tablespoons sugar gradually, beating constantly until stiff peaks form. Spread over the filling, sealing to the edge. Bake at 325 degrees for 10 to 12 minutes or until golden brown. **Yield:** 8 servings.

PER SERVING:
CALORIES: 215; CARBOHYDRATE: 40 g; PROTEIN: 6.7 g; TOTAL FAT: 3 g;
CHOLESTEROL: 1 mg; SODIUM: 216 mg; FIBER: trace;
CALORIES FROM FAT: 21%

Pumpkin Pie

1 (16-ounce) can pumpkin
4 egg whites, lightly beaten
1 (12-ounce) can evaporated skim milk
¾ cup sugar
1 teaspoon cinnamon
½ teaspoon vanilla extract
½ teaspoon ginger
¼ teaspoon ground cloves
¼ teaspoon cardamom
¼ teaspoon allspice
¼ teaspoon nutmeg
4 teaspoons sugar
¼ teaspoon pumpkin pie spice
4 sheets phyllo dough

Spray a 9-inch pie plate with nonstick cooking spray. Combine the pumpkin and egg whites in a bowl and mix well. Add the evaporated skim milk, ¾ cup sugar, cinnamon, vanilla, ginger, cloves, cardamom, allspice and nutmeg and mix well. Combine 4 teaspoons sugar and the pumpkin pie spice in a small bowl and mix well. Stack the phyllo dough; cut in half to make 8 sheets. Cover with a tea towel to prevent drying out. Place 1 sheet of the phyllo in the pie plate. Spray with butter-flavor nonstick cooking spray; sprinkle with ½ teaspoon of the pumpkin pie spice mixture. Repeat the procedure with the remaining phyllo dough and pumpkin pie spice mixture, fanning the phyllo sheets evenly until the entire pie plate rim is covered. Spoon the pumpkin filling into the phyllo shell; trim excess dough from edge. Cover edge loosely with foil to prevent burning. Bake at 425 degrees for 13 minutes. Reduce oven temperature to 350 degrees. Bake for 40 to 50 minutes longer or until set. Remove to a wire rack to cool. **Yield:** 8 servings.

Per Serving:
CALORIES: 178; CARBOHYDRATE: 30.7 g; PROTEIN: 5.8 g; TOTAL FAT: trace;
CHOLESTEROL: 1.5 mg; SODIUM: 72 mg; FIBER: trace;
CALORIES FROM FAT: 0%

SAINTLY DELIGHTS

Low-Fat Pie Crust

½ cup all-purpose flour
½ cup whole wheat flour
¼ teaspoon salt
¼ cup reduced-calorie margarine
2 tablespoons cold water

Sift the all-purpose flour, whole wheat flour and salt into a bowl and mix well. Cut in the margarine until crumbly. Add the cold water, stirring until of the desired consistency; dough will be crumbly. Shape into a ball. Place the dough between 2 sheets of heavy-duty plastic wrap; press into a 4-inch circle. Chill for 20 minutes. Roll the dough into a 12-inch circle. Freeze for 5 minutes or until the plastic wrap can be easily removed. Remove top sheet of plastic wrap. Invert and fit into a 9-inch pie plate; remove the remaining sheet of plastic wrap. Fold the pastry edge under and flute; seal to edge of pie plate. Prick the bottom and sides of the pastry with a fork. Bake at 400 degrees for 10 minutes or until light brown. Remove to a wire rack to cool. **Yield:** 8 servings.

PER SERVING:
CALORIES: 79; CARBOHYDRATE: 11.4 g; PROTEIN: 1.8 g; TOTAL FAT: 2.5 g;
CHOLESTEROL: 0 mg; SODIUM: 137 mg; FIBER: trace;
CALORIES FROM FAT: 29%

SAINTLY DELIGHTS

APPLESAUCE BREAD PUDDING

1 (16-ounce) loaf light white bread ♦ 1 cup raisins
2 teaspoons cinnamon ♦ 2 cups skim milk
1 cup no-sugar-added applesauce ♦ 8 egg whites
½ cup packed brown sugar ♦ 1½ teaspoons vanilla extract

Cut the bread slices into ½-inch cubes. Toss the bread, raisins and cinnamon in a bowl. Beat the skim milk, applesauce, egg whites, brown sugar and vanilla in a bowl until mixed. Pour over the bread cube mixture. Let stand for 25 minutes. Spoon into an 8x8-inch baking dish sprayed with nonstick cooking spray. Bake at 350 degrees for 35 to 40 minutes or until a knife inserted in the center comes out clean. Let stand for 15 to 20 minutes before serving. **Yield:** 8 servings.

PER SERVING:
CALORIES: 231; CARBOHYDRATE: 53.3 g; PROTEIN: 11 g; TOTAL FAT: 0.7 g;
CHOLESTEROL: 0.8 mg; SODIUM: 328 mg; FIBER: trace;
CALORIES FROM FAT: 3%

RICE PUDDING

1 cup egg substitute ♦ 2 egg whites
¾ cup sugar or 3 teaspoons Sweet 'n Low
1¾ cups skim milk ♦ 2 cups cooked rice
½ cup raisins
1 teaspoon cinnamon ♦ ¼ teaspoon nutmeg

Combine the egg substitute and egg whites in a bowl. Beat with a whisk until frothy. Add the sugar, beating until blended. Stir in the skim milk, rice, raisins, cinnamon and nutmeg. Spoon into a baking dish. Bake at 400 degrees for 45 minutes. **Yield:** 8 servings.

PER SERVING:
CALORIES: 202; CARBOHYDRATE: 43.6 g; PROTEIN: 6.9 g; TOTAL FAT: 0.3 g;
CHOLESTEROL: 0.9 mg; SODIUM: 83 mg; FIBER: trace;
CALORIES FROM FAT: 1%

SAINTLY DELIGHTS

Pasta Magnifico

Pasta has become an American menu mainstay during the last decade, and there are few people—even in the deep South—who can't tell you the difference between fettuccini, spaghetti, and penne.

Our collective desire for pasta dishes has grown for many reasons. Busy households (whose isn't?) have found that there are few dishes as versatile and as quick to prepare as a pasta entrée. Plus it's easy to personalize a dish with the ingredients on hand. A little olive oil, some fresh herbs and tomatoes, a fresh, sautéed vegetable, a few grinds of the pepper mill, shake on some grated cheese, and you've got a meal.

Our choices are wider-ranging nowadays, too. Better make sure that you skip the old-fashioned Fettuccini Alfredo. Recently, a consumer group whose mission is to inform the public of the dangers of poor eating habits described this dish as "a heart attack on a plate"!

Make sure that your personal definition of "magnificent" means that the pasta dish you've selected can't be described in such a manner. These selections will ensure that doesn't happen.

Nashville riverfront and the H. G. Hill Steamboat *that traversed the Cumberland River for only a few years in the early 1920s. Inset: Nashville's Riverfront Park and skyline in 1996.*

WILES
NASHVILLE, TEN

Fettuccini Alfredo Then

1 cup whipping cream
¼ cup butter, softened
2 tablespoons
parsley flakes
1 teaspoon pepper
⅔ cup boiling water
8 ounces fettuccini
1 clove of garlic, minced
¼ cup butter
½ cup grated
Romano cheese

Per Serving:
Calories: 744;
Carbohydrate: 44 g;
Protein: 18 g;
Total Fat: 56 g;
Cholesterol: 179 mg;
Sodium: 613 mg;
Fiber: trace;
Calories from Fat: 68%

Pasta Magnifico

Fettuccini Alfredo Now

2 small cloves of garlic, minced
1 tablespoon margarine
1 tablespoon flour
1⅓ cups skim milk
2 tablespoons light cream cheese
1 cup grated fresh Parmesan cheese
4 cups hot cooked fettuccini
1 tablespoon chopped fresh parsley
Freshly ground pepper to taste
Grated fat-free Parmesan cheese to taste

Sauté the garlic in the margarine in a saucepan over medium heat for 1 minute. Stir in the flour. Add the milk gradually, stirring constantly. Cook for 8 minutes or until thickened, stirring constantly. Stir in the cream cheese. Cook for 2 minutes, stirring constantly. Add 1 cup Parmesan cheese. Cook until blended, stirring constantly. Spoon over the fettuccini in a serving bowl, tossing to coat. Sprinkle with the parsley, pepper and Parmesan cheese to taste. Cook the fettuccini without added salt or oil. **Yield:** 4 (1 cup) servings.

Per Serving:
Calories: 331; Carbohydrate: 36 g; Protein: 12.7 g; Total Fat: 8.8 g;
Cholesterol: 18 mg; Sodium: 401 mg; Fiber: trace;
Calories from Fat: 24%

Angel Hair Pasta with Chicken, Asparagus and Roasted Red Pepper Sauce

2 chicken breast halves, skinned
2 medium to large red bell peppers, roasted, skinned, chopped
2 tablespoons chopped onion ♦ 1 teaspoon minced garlic
½ teaspoon chopped fresh basil ♦ Salt and black pepper to taste
Cayenne to taste ♦ 2 tablespoons olive oil
1 tablespoon skim milk ♦ ⅓ teaspoon cornstarch
¾ cup chicken stock, skimmed
2 cups cooked angel hair pasta
10 to 12 fresh asparagus spears, steamed
2 fresh mushroom caps, steamed

Rinse the chicken and pat dry. Trim any visible fat. Cut into small pieces. Sauté the red peppers, onion, garlic, basil, salt, pepper and cayenne in 1 tablespoon of the olive oil in a saucepan over high heat for 3 to 4 minutes. Combine the remaining 1 tablespoon olive oil, skim milk and cornstarch in a bowl or blender and mix well. (This mixture helps to thicken and smooth out the flavor of the sauce, as well as acting as a substitute for whipping cream.) Combine the cornstarch mixture, red pepper mixture and ½ cup of the chicken stock in a saucepan. Simmer for 8 to 10 minutes, stirring frequently. Process in a blender or food processor until puréed and of sauce consistency. Transfer to a clean saucepan. Adjust the seasonings. Cover and keep warm. Sauté the chicken in the remaining ¼ cup chicken stock in a skillet until cooked through. Arrange the pasta on 2 dinner plates. Top with the chicken, asparagus and mushrooms. Drizzle with the warm red pepper sauce. **Yield:** 2 servings.

Per Serving:
Calories: 540; Carbohydrate: 63 g; Protein: 33 g; Total Fat: 18 g;
Cholesterol: 55 mg; Sodium: 163 mg; Fiber: trace;
Calories from Fat: 30%

Roasted Red Peppers

Arrange red bell peppers on a baking sheet. Roast at 375 degrees until blistered and charred on all sides, turning frequently. Wrap the red peppers in plastic wrap. Cool in the refrigerator or in an ice water bath. Peel, seed, and coarsely chop the red peppers when cool.

Pasta Magnifico

Black Bean Pasta

1 large onion, sliced
1 small red bell pepper, cut into strips
1 yellow bell pepper, cut into strips
8 ounces fresh mushrooms, sliced
2 tablespoons olive oil
1 (15-ounce) can black beans, drained, rinsed
1 (16-ounce) can whole tomatoes, chopped
1 (15½-ounce) can kidney beans
1½ ounces capers, drained
¼ cup sliced black olives
¼ teaspoon rosemary
¼ teaspoon basil
¼ teaspoon pepper
12 ounces angel hair pasta, cooked, drained

Sauté the onion, red pepper, yellow pepper and mushrooms in the olive oil in a skillet over medium-high heat until tender. Stir in the black beans, undrained tomatoes, undrained kidney beans, capers, black olives, rosemary, basil and pepper. Bring to a boil; reduce heat. Simmer for 30 minutes, stirring occasionally. Spoon over the angel hair pasta on a serving platter. Garnish with freshly grated fat-free Parmesan cheese and basil leaves. **Yield:** 6 servings.

Per Serving:
Calories: 393; Carbohydrate: 66 g; Protein: 17 g; Total Fat: 7.5 g;
Cholesterol: 0 mg; Sodium: 378 mg; Fiber: 3.5 g;
Calories from Fat: 17%

Pasta Magnifico

Creamy Chicken Basil Pasta

½ cup fat-free mayonnaise
¼ cup fat-free sour cream
2 tablespoons chopped fresh basil
2 tablespoons skim milk
1 tablespoon lemon juice
¼ teaspoon garlic powder
¼ teaspoon dry mustard
1 cup fresh broccoli florets
½ cup frozen peas, thawed
4 cups cooked fettuccini
3 cups chopped cooked skinless chicken breast
4 ounces low-fat Cheddar cheese, cut into thin strips
1 cup chopped tomato
½ medium red bell pepper, julienned
¼ cup sliced green onions

Combine the mayonnaise, sour cream, basil, skim milk, lemon juice, garlic powder and dry mustard in a bowl and mix well. Arrange the broccoli and peas in a vegetable steamer. Steam, covered, over boiling water for 3 minutes or until tender-crisp; drain. Rinse under cold water until cool; drain. Combine the mayonnaise mixture, broccoli, peas, fettuccini, chicken, Cheddar cheese, tomato, red pepper and green onions in a large bowl, tossing to mix. Chill, covered, until serving time. Cook the fettuccini and chicken without added salt. **Yield:** 8 servings.

PER SERVING:
CALORIES: 282; CARBOHYDRATE: 28 g; PROTEIN: 28 g; TOTAL FAT: 5.5 g;
CHOLESTEROL: 60 mg; SODIUM: 366 mg; FIBER: 2 g;
CALORIES FROM FAT: 18%

Strength training is a MUST for you! Everyone who is medically allowed to lift weights should do so. Use elastic bands or cans of food.

PASTA MAGNIFICO

Low-Fat Vegetable Lasagna

9 lasagna noodles ♦ 1 teaspoon vegetable oil
1 cup chopped yellow onion ♦ 2 cloves of garlic, crushed
8 ounces fresh mushrooms, thinly sliced
¼ cup chopped fresh parsley (optional) ♦ Salt to taste
1 (10-ounce) package frozen spinach, thawed, drained
2 cups meatless tomato or spaghetti sauce ♦ 1 teaspoon oregano
1 teaspoon basil ♦ 15 ounces part-skim or low-fat ricotta cheese
¾ cup shredded part-skim mozzarella cheese
2 tablespoons grated Parmesan cheese

Cook the lasagna noodles using package directions. Drain and pat dry with paper towels. Heat the oil in a nonstick skillet over medium heat until hot. Cook the onion in the oil for 5 minutes or until golden brown. Add the garlic. Cook for 1 minute. Transfer ½ of the onion mixture to a bowl. Stir the mushrooms into the remaining onion mixture. Cook over medium heat for 7 minutes or until the mushrooms are tender and light brown, stirring frequently. Stir in the parsley and salt. Transfer to a bowl. Add the reserved onion mixture and spinach to the skillet. Cook, covered, for 3 minutes or until the spinach wilts; remove cover. Cook for 1 minute or until all moisture evaporates, stirring frequently. Mix the tomato sauce, oregano and basil in a bowl. Spread ½ of the tomato sauce mixture in a 9x13-inch baking dish sprayed with nonstick cooking spray. Arrange 3 lasagna noodles slightly overlapping over the sauce. Spread with the spinach mixture, ½ of the ricotta cheese and ¼ cup of the mozzarella cheese in the order listed. Layer 3 lasagna noodles, mushroom mixture, remaining ricotta cheese and ¼ cup of the mozzarella cheese in the order listed over the prepared layers. Top with the remaining lasagna noodles and remaining tomato sauce. Sprinkle with the remaining mozzarella cheese and the Parmesan cheese. Bake at 350 degrees for 45 minutes or until bubbly. **Yield:** 6 servings.

Per Serving:
Calories: 361; Carbohydrate: 46 g; Protein: 24 g; Total Fat: 5.9 g;
Cholesterol: 33 mg; Sodium: 222 mg; Fiber: trace;
Calories from Fat: 15%

Linguini with Clam Sauce

1 (8-ounce) can minced clams
1 tablespoon olive oil
1 medium onion, chopped
2 cloves of garlic, minced
¼ cup white wine or cider
Juice of 1 lemon
½ teaspoon pepper
2 tablespoons chopped pimento
8 ounces cholesterol-free linguini or angel hair pasta
¼ cup chopped fresh parsley, basil or oregano

Drain the clams, reserving the liquid. Heat the olive oil in a skillet until hot. Add the onion and garlic. Sauté for 2 to 3 minutes. Stir in the reserved clam juice and white wine. Cook over medium heat for 15 minutes or until reduced by ½, stirring frequently; reduce heat. Stir in the clams, lemon juice and pepper. Simmer, covered, for 5 minutes, stirring occasionally. Add the pimento and mix well. Remove from heat. Cook the pasta using package directions; drain. Add the pasta to the clam mixture and mix well. Stir in the parsley. Cook for 5 to 8 minutes or until heated through, stirring frequently. May substitute oysters for the clams. **Yield:** 4 servings.

Per Serving:
Calories: 297; Carbohydrate: 36.4 g; Protein: 18.8 g; Total Fat: 5.7 g;
Cholesterol: 38 mg; Sodium: 66 mg; Fiber: trace;
Calories from Fat: 17%

Tossing cooked pasta in a little chicken stock before adding the sauce lends the same silky texture to the pasta as would olive oil, with none of the fat.

Pasta Magnifico

PASTA MAGNIFICO

CHICKEN LINGUINI

16 ounces linguini
4 chicken breasts, skinned, boned
1 pound fresh mushrooms, sliced
½ cup dry sherry or white wine ♦ ½ cup chopped onion
3 cups canned no-salt-added chicken broth
¼ cup plus 2 tablespoons flour
1 cup nonfat sour cream
½ cup shredded low-fat Monterey Jack cheese
¼ cup plus 2 tablespoons freshly grated fat-free Parmesan cheese
⅛ teaspoon freshly ground pepper
¼ cup fine dry bread crumbs
1 tablespoon reduced-calorie margarine

Cook the pasta using package directions, omitting the salt and fat; drain. Rinse the chicken. Combine the chicken with enough water to cover in a saucepan. Bring to a boil; reduce heat. Simmer, covered, for 20 minutes or until cooked through; drain. Cool slightly and shred. Sauté the mushrooms in the sherry in a nonstick skillet sprayed with butter-flavor nonstick cooking spray for 5 minutes. Spray a saucepan with nonstick cooking spray. Heat over medium heat until hot. Sauté the onion in the prepared saucepan until tender. Combine ½ cup of the broth and flour in a bowl and mix well. Add the flour mixture and remaining broth to the onion. Cook over medium heat until thickened, stirring constantly. Remove from heat. Stir in the sour cream. Combine the mushroom mixture, chicken, sour cream mixture, Monterey Jack cheese, ¼ cup of the Parmesan cheese and pepper in a bowl and mix well. Add the pasta and mix well. Spoon into a 9x13-inch baking dish sprayed with nonstick cooking spray. Combine the bread crumbs, remaining Parmesan cheese and margarine in a bowl and mix well. Sprinkle over the prepared layer. Bake at 350 degrees for 30 minutes. **Yield:** 10 servings.

PER SERVING:
CALORIES: 338; CARBOHYDRATE: 48 g; PROTEIN: 23 g; TOTAL FAT: 5 g;
CHOLESTEROL: 32 mg; SODIUM: 183 mg; FIBER: 2 g;
CALORIES FROM FAT: 12%

Garlic Shrimp and Scallop Sauce

1 teaspoon olive oil
2 tablespoons slivered garlic
½ teaspoon red pepper flakes, crushed
8 ounces large shrimp, peeled, deveined
8 ounces bay scallops
½ teaspoon paprika
¼ cup low-sodium chicken broth
1 teaspoon fresh lime juice
½ cup finely chopped fresh Italian parsley
⅛ teaspoon salt
Freshly ground black pepper to taste

Heat the olive oil in a heavy skillet over medium heat until hot. Add the garlic. Sauté just until light brown. Remove the garlic with a slotted spoon to a bowl. Add the red pepper flakes to the skillet; increase the heat to medium-high. Add the garlic, shrimp, scallops and paprika to the skillet. Sauté for 1 to 2 minutes. Stir in the broth. Cook for 1 minute, stirring frequently. Remove the shrimp and scallops with a slotted spoon to a bowl. Add the lime juice, parsley, salt and black pepper to the skillet. Cook just until heated through. Pour over the shrimp and scallops and mix well. Serve over hot cooked linguini or fettuccini. **Yield:** 4 servings.

Per Serving:
Calories: 137; Carbohydrate: 5 g; Protein: 22 g; Total Fat: 3 g;
Cholesterol: 105 mg; Sodium: 264 mg; Fiber: trace;
Calories from Fat: 19%

Pasta Magnifico

SUPER-EASY MANICOTTI WITH CHEESE

1 (32-ounce) jar no-salt-added spaghetti sauce
1 cup water
2 cups fat-free ricotta cheese
2 cups shredded low-fat mozzarella cheese
¼ cup grated fat-free Parmesan cheese
1 tablespoon chopped fresh parsley
¼ teaspoon pepper
8 ounces uncooked manicotti

Combine the spaghetti sauce and water in a saucepan and mix well. Bring to a boil; reduce heat. Cover to keep warm. Combine the ricotta cheese, mozzarella cheese, Parmesan cheese, parsley and pepper in a bowl and mix well. Stuff the manicotti shells with the cheese mixture. Spread 1 cup of the warm spaghetti sauce over the bottom of a 9x13-inch baking dish. Arrange the stuffed manicotti shells in a single layer over the sauce. Pour the remaining spaghetti sauce over the pasta shells. Bake, covered with foil, at 400 degrees for 40 minutes or until bubbly; remove the foil. Bake for 10 minutes longer. **Yield:** 8 servings.

PER SERVING:
CALORIES: 332; CARBOHYDRATE: 35.9 g; PROTEIN: 22.9 g; TOTAL FAT: 10.4 g;
CHOLESTEROL: 36 mg; SODIUM: 252 mg; FIBER: trace;
CALORIES FROM FAT: 28%

PASTA MAGNIFICO

Fresh Tomato and Herb Primavera Pasta Sauce

2 medium to large tomatoes, finely chopped
⅓ cup chopped green onions
2 tablespoons finely chopped fresh parsley
6 cloves of garlic, minced
2 teaspoons olive oil
½ teaspoon basil
½ teaspoon oregano
¼ teaspoon salt
¼ teaspoon pepper
Juice of ½ lemon
1 cup chopped peeled eggplant
1 cup chopped zucchini
1 cup chopped yellow squash
1 small onion, chopped

Combine the tomatoes, green onions, parsley, ½ of the garlic, 1 teaspoon of the olive oil, basil, oregano, salt, pepper and lemon juice in a bowl and mix gently. Let stand for 1 hour for flavors to marry. Spray a large skillet with nonstick cooking spray. Heat until hot. Add the remaining olive oil, remaining garlic, eggplant, zucchini, yellow squash and onion to the skillet. Sauté until the vegetables are tender-crisp. Stir in the tomato mixture. Cook for 2 to 3 minutes or until heated through, stirring frequently. Serve over your favorite hot cooked pasta. **Yield:** 6 (¾-cup) servings.

Per Serving:
Calories: 42; Carbohydrate: 7.3 g; Protein: 1.5 g; Total Fat: 1.4 g;
Cholesterol: 0 mg; Sodium: 102 mg; Fiber: trace;
Calories from Fat: 30%

Fresh Tomato Marinara Sauce

Sauté 1 chopped small onion and 2 minced cloves of garlic in a skillet sprayed with nonstick cooking spray. Deglaze with ⅓ cup skimmed low-sodium chicken broth. Stir in ¾ cup chopped fresh or canned no-salt-added tomatoes, 6 ounces no-salt-added tomato sauce and 1 teaspoon tomato paste. Simmer until heated through. Season with basil, oregano and pepper to taste.

Pasta Magnifico

American home life has changed drastically during the 1980s and 1990s. Even residents of small towns in the South now have daily schedules that require all sorts of juggling and balancing. We once sat down together three times a day to spend family time and talk about our activities. These days, it seems that everyone in the household is heading in a different direction at a pre-appointed time and rarely do our schedules intersect.

But many households are attempting to set some ground rules. We've had two-career families long enough now to realize that perhaps a little balance is in order. Maybe we should plan what is commonly called "quality time" to be with our families and spend time with each other. As our work lives become more complex and the world around us changes so rapidly that we're unable to absorb the impact on our lives, many people are deciding that no matter how many different directions we're heading in, we'd better build in some time that we can share. Most often that means the evening meal, dinner or "supper" depending on your own personal description. Here are some suggestions on how to make the main event of your daily meals a special time for you and your family.

Ryman Auditorium, built in 1892, housed the Grand Ole Opry from 1941 until 1974. Inset: Ryman Auditorium in 1996 continues to host entertainment that supports Nashville's identity as Music City.

THE MAIN
EVENT

CHICKEN BREASTS IN WINE THEN

½ cup melted butter
Chopped green onions
4 whole chicken
breasts, split
Salt and pepper to taste
½ cup marsala
1 cup whipping cream
1 cup sliced fresh
mushrooms
1 teaspoon paprika
Sliced black olives

PER SERVING:
CALORIES: 453;
CARBOHYDRATE: 4 g;
PROTEIN: 32 g;
TOTAL FAT: 33 g;
CHOLESTEROL: 163 mg;
SODIUM: 427 mg;
FIBER: trace;
CALORIES FROM FAT: 66%

THE MAIN EVENT

CHICKEN BREASTS WITH SHERRIED MUSHROOMS NOW

4 (4-ounce) boneless skinless chicken breast halves
1 (10½-ounce) can low-sodium chicken broth
2 tablespoons flour ♦ ⅛ teaspoon salt ♦ ¼ teaspoon pepper
2 cups sliced fresh mushrooms
2 tablespoons minced green onions
1 tablespoon melted reduced-calorie margarine
¼ cup dry sherry or white wine ♦ 1½ teaspoons cornstarch
1 tablespoon chopped fresh parsley

Rinse the chicken and pat dry. Boil the broth in a saucepan for 5 minutes or until reduced to 1 cup. Sprinkle the chicken with a mixture of the flour, salt and pepper. Cook in a nonstick skillet sprayed with nonstick cooking spray over medium-high heat for 5 minutes on each side or until brown. Remove from skillet. Wipe the skillet dry. Sauté the mushrooms and green onions in the margarine in the skillet. Stir in the broth and 3 tablespoons of the sherry. Bring to a boil. Cook until reduced to ¾ cup. Stir in a mixture of the remaining sherry and cornstarch. Cook for 1 minute or until thickened, stirring constantly; reduce heat. Add the chicken. Simmer, covered, for 10 minutes or until cooked through. Arrange the chicken on a serving platter; top with the mushroom mixture. Sprinkle with the parsley. **Yield:** 4 servings.

PER SERVING:
CALORIES: 197; CARBOHYDRATE: 7 g; PROTEIN: 28.4 g; TOTAL FAT: 5.6 g;
CHOLESTEROL: 72 mg; SODIUM: 194 mg; FIBER: trace;
CALORIES FROM FAT: 26%

Braised Sirloin Tips

2 pounds beef sirloin tips
½ teaspoon unseasoned meat tenderizer
¼ teaspoon freshly ground pepper
½ cup finely chopped onion
2 cloves of garlic, finely minced
1¼ cups low-sodium beef broth
⅓ cup dry red wine
1 tablespoon light soy sauce
¼ cup cold water
2 tablespoons cornstarch
¼ cup minced fresh parsley

Remove all visible fat from the sirloin tips; cut into cubes. Drain on paper towels. Sprinkle the meat tenderizer and pepper on all sides of the beef. Cook in a large nonstick skillet over medium-high heat until brown on all sides. Add the onion and garlic to the skillet. Cook until the onion is tender. Stir in the broth, red wine and soy sauce. Bring to a boil; reduce heat. Simmer, covered, for 1½ hours or until the beef is tender, stirring occasionally. Add a mixture of the water and cornstarch gradually, stirring constantly. Cook until thickened, stirring constantly. Spoon onto a serving platter; sprinkle with the parsley. Serve with hot cooked rice. **Yield:** 8 servings.

Per Serving:
Calories: 177; Carbohydrate: 5 g; Protein: 26 g; Total Fat: 5 g;
Cholesterol: 67 mg; Sodium: 244 mg; Fiber: trace;
Calories from Fat: 25%

Dry wine makes a great marinade. The acid content of wine helps break down fibers, tenderizing inexpensive, tougher cuts of lean meats.

The Main Event

155

Pork Medallions with Sweet Peppers

¼ cup flour
¼ teaspoon whole basil
⅛ teaspoon salt
⅛ teaspoon pepper
1 pound pork medallions
Julienne strips of red, yellow and green bell peppers
3 tablespoons dry white wine
Fresh basil sprigs

Combine the flour, basil, salt and pepper in a shallow bowl and mix well. Coat the pork with the flour mixture. Spray a large nonstick skillet with nonstick cooking spray. Heat over medium-high heat until hot. Add the pork to the skillet. Cook for 4 to 5 minutes on each side or until cooked through, stirring frequently. Drain and pat dry. Arrange on a serving platter. Cover to keep warm. Wipe the drippings from the skillet with a paper towel. Spray the skillet with nonstick cooking spray. Sauté the red, yellow and green peppers in the prepared skillet over medium-high heat for 5 to 7 minutes or until tender-crisp. Stir in the white wine. Arrange around the pork; sprinkle with basil sprigs. **Yield:** 4 servings.

PER SERVING:
CALORIES: 210; CARBOHYDRATE: 7.7 g; PROTEIN: 29.8 g; TOTAL FAT: 4.9 g;
CHOLESTEROL: 93 mg; SODIUM: 140 mg; FIBER: trace;
CALORIES FROM FAT: 21%

THE MAIN EVENT

Apricot Olive Chicken Breasts

6 chicken breast halves, skinned, boned
1 cup chopped dried apricots
10 green olives, cut into halves
¼ cup red wine vinegar
2 large cloves of garlic, minced
2 tablespoons oregano
1 tablespoon capers
¼ teaspoon pepper
1 bay leaf
⅓ cup packed brown sugar
¾ cup white wine

Rinse the chicken and pat dry. Spray lightly with olive oil- flavor nonstick cooking spray. Arrange in a shallow baking dish. Combine the apricots, olives, wine vinegar, garlic, oregano, capers, pepper and bay leaf in a bowl and mix well. Pour over the chicken, turning to coat. Marinate in the refrigerator for 8 to 10 hours, turning occasionally. Sprinkle with the brown sugar; pour the white wine over the chicken. Bake at 375 degrees for 40 to 45 minutes or until the chicken is cooked through. Discard the bay leaf. May substitute prunes for the apricots. **Yield:** 6 servings.

Per Serving:
Calories: 250; Carbohydrate: 22 g; Protein: 21.4 g; Total Fat: 3.9 g;
Cholesterol: 73 mg; Sodium: 202 mg; Fiber: trace;
Calories from Fat: 14%

The Main Event

Parmesan Chicken Strips

8 (4-ounce) chicken breast halves, skinned, boned
¼ cup skim milk
¼ cup frozen egg substitute, thawed
⅔ cup fine dry bread crumbs
⅔ cup grated fat-free Parmesan cheese
1¼ teaspoons whole basil
¾ teaspoon whole thyme
¼ teaspoon onion powder
¼ teaspoon freshly ground pepper

Rinse the chicken and pat dry. Cut into 1x4-inch strips. Combine the skim milk and egg substitute in a bowl and mix well. Combine the bread crumbs, Parmesan cheese, basil, thyme, onion powder and pepper in a shallow dish and mix well. Dip the chicken in the milk mixture; roll in the bread crumb mixture. Arrange on a baking sheet sprayed with nonstick cooking spray. Bake at 400 degrees for 18 minutes or until cooked through and light brown. **Yield:** 8 servings.

Per Serving:
Calories: 197; Carbohydrate: 8.3 g; Protein: 30.2 g; Total Fat: 3.5 g;
Cholesterol: 73.3 mg; Sodium: 189 mg; Fiber: 0 g;
Calories from Fat: 16%

CHICKEN GUMBO

1½ cups cooked okra
1 onion, finely chopped
½ green bell pepper, finely chopped
4 cups low-sodium chicken stock, skimmed
2½ cups canned stewed no-salt-added tomatoes
1 small bay leaf
Salt and pepper to taste
1 cup finely chopped cooked chicken breast
1 tablespoon minced fresh parsley

Spray a saucepan with butter-flavor nonstick cooking spray. Sauté the okra, onion and green pepper in the prepared saucepan until golden brown. Stir in the stock, tomatoes and bay leaf. Simmer over low heat for 45 minutes, stirring occasionally. Stir in salt and pepper. Discard the bay leaf. Stir in the chicken and parsley 15 minutes before serving. **Yield:** 6 servings.

PER SERVING:
CALORIES: 98; CARBOHYDRATE: 9 g; PROTEIN: 13 g; TOTAL FAT: 1 g;
CHOLESTEROL: 25 mg; SODIUM: 71 mg; FIBER: trace;
CALORIES FROM FAT: 13%

Take the focus off small meat portions by trying stir-fry. This uses very little oil and lots of vegetables.

THE MAIN EVENT

CREAMY CHICKEN, LEEK AND MUSHROOM SOUP

1 pound boneless skinless chicken breasts
3 cups (3 medium) chopped leeks
3 cloves of garlic, minced
4 cups (12-ounces) quartered fresh mushrooms
3 cups low-fat no-salt-added chicken broth
⅓ cup chablis or other dry white wine
½ cup flour
2½ cups ½% milk
2 tablespoons medium dry sherry
¼ teaspoon salt
¼ teaspoon pepper

Rinse the chicken and pat dry. Cut into bite-size pieces. Spray a large heavy saucepan with nonstick cooking spray. Heat over medium-high heat until hot. Add the chicken, leeks and garlic to the prepared skillet. Sauté for 10 minutes. Stir in the mushrooms. Sauté for 5 minutes. Add the broth and white wine and mix well. Bring to a boil; reduce heat. Simmer for 10 minutes, stirring occasionally. Place the flour in a small bowl. Add the milk gradually, whisking constantly until blended. Stir into the chicken mixture. Cook over medium heat for 10 minutes or until thickened, stirring constantly. Stir in the sherry, salt and pepper. Ladle into soup bowls.
Yield: 6 (1½-cup) servings.

Per Serving:
Calories: 235; Carbohydrate: 23.6 g; Protein: 25.4 g; Total Fat: 3.3 g;
Cholesterol: 53.2 mg; Sodium: 230 mg; Fiber: trace;
Calories from Fat: 13%

THE MAIN EVENT

Turkey Cutlet Fricassee

4 (4-ounce) skinless turkey breast cutlets
⅛ teaspoon pepper
1½ cups water
1⅓ cups diagonally sliced carrots
1 cup coarsely chopped onion
1 cup frozen whole kernel corn
8 ounces sliced fresh mushrooms
¼ cup chablis or other dry white wine (optional)
½ teaspoon chicken bouillon granules
½ teaspoon whole tarragon
½ teaspoon whole thyme
1 bay leaf
½ cup evaporated skim milk
2 tablespoon cornstarch
1 teaspoon lemon juice
Fresh tarragon sprigs (optional)

Rinse the turkey and pat dry. Sprinkle the cutlets with the pepper. Spray a large heavy saucepan with nonstick cooking spray. Heat over medium-high heat until hot. Add the cutlets to the prepared saucepan. Cook for 2 minutes on each side or until brown. Add the water, carrots, onion, corn, mushrooms, white wine, bouillon granules, tarragon, thyme and bay leaf and mix well. Bring to a boil; reduce heat. Simmer, covered, for 15 minutes or until the turkey is cooked through. Transfer the cutlets to a serving platter. Combine the evaporated skim milk and cornstarch in a bowl and mix well. Stir into the vegetable mixture. Bring to a boil; reduce heat. Simmer until thickened, stirring constantly. Remove from heat. Stir in the lemon juice. Discard the bay leaf. Spoon the vegetable mixture around the turkey cutlets. Top with the tarragon sprigs. **Yield:** 4 servings.

Per Serving:
Calories: 251; Carbohydrate: 26.6 g; Protein: 32 g; Total Fat: 2.2 g;
Cholesterol: 67 mg; Sodium: 235 mg; Fiber: 4.2 g;
Calories from Fat: 8%

The Main Event

CURRIED TURKEY WITH WATER CHESTNUTS

1 bunch green onions
1 small rib celery
1 green bell pepper, sliced
2 cups thinly sliced water chestnuts
2 cups chopped cooked turkey
2 tablespoons slivered almonds
3 tablespoons flour
1 teaspoon curry powder
1 teaspoon paprika
½ teaspoon basil
1½ cups low-sodium chicken broth, skimmed
1 cup drained pineapple tidbits
¼ cup chopped pimento
Pepper to taste

Cut the green onions and celery diagonally into ½-inch slices. Spray a skillet with nonstick cooking spray. Sauté the green onions, celery and green pepper in the prepared skillet until light brown. Add the water chestnuts, turkey and almonds and mix well. Stir in a mixture of the flour, curry powder, paprika and basil. Sauté until well blended. Stir in the broth, pineapple and pimento. Steam, covered, until heated through. Season with pepper. May substitute chicken for the turkey. **Yield:** 6 servings.

PER SERVING:
CALORIES: 166; CARBOHYDRATE: 19.8 g; PROTEIN: 14.5 g; TOTAL FAT: 3.9 g;
CHOLESTEROL: 25.3 mg; SODIUM: 56 mg; FIBER: trace;
CALORIES FROM FAT: 21%

Annie's Baked Grouper

4 slices whole wheat bread, crumbled
¼ cup grated fat-free Parmesan cheese
2 teaspoons chopped fresh parsley
½ teaspoon thyme
1 pound grouper fillets
Paprika to taste
Pepper to taste

Combine the bread crumbs, Parmesan cheese, parsley and thyme in a bowl and mix well. Sprinkle in an 8x8-inch baking dish sprayed with nonstick cooking spray. Arrange the fillets in the prepared dish. Spray with nonstick cooking spray. Sprinkle with the paprika and pepper. Bake at 375 degrees for 15 minutes or until the fish flakes easily. **Yield:** 3 servings.

Per Serving:
Calories: 253; Carbohydrate: 21 g; Protein: 35.5 g; Total Fat: 2.8 g;
Cholesterol: 58 mg; Sodium: 392 mg; Fiber: trace;
Calories from Fat: 10%

Cooking meat for a longer time allows for more loss of fat, so medium- and well-done meats are preferred over rare.

The Main Event

Oven-Fried Fish

¼ cup cornmeal
¼ cup fine dry bread crumbs
½ teaspoon paprika
¼ teaspoon salt
¼ teaspoon dillweed
⅛ teaspoon pepper
1 pound grouper or orange roughy fillets, cut into 1-inch strips
⅓ cup skim milk
Italian parsley sprigs
Lemon halves

Combine the cornmeal, bread crumbs, paprika, salt, dillweed and pepper in a shallow dish and mix well. Dip the fillets in the skim milk; coat with the cornmeal mixture. Arrange in a 9x13-inch baking dish sprayed with nonstick cooking spray. Spray with fat-free spray margarine. Bake at 450 degrees for 10 minutes or until the fish flakes easily. Arrange the fish on a serving platter. Top with Italian parsley. Wrap lemon halves in cheesecloth and arrange around the fish.
Yield: 4 servings.

Per Serving:
Calories: 192; Carbohydrate: 12 g; Protein: 24 g; Total Fat: 4.4 g;
Cholesterol: 42 mg; Sodium: 288 mg; Fiber: trace;
Calories from Fat: 21%

The Main Event

WINE-HERB HALIBUT STEAK

4 (1-inch-thick) halibut steaks
½ cup chablis or other dry white wine
1 tablespoon lemon juice
¼ teaspoon basil
¼ teaspoon oregano
¼ teaspoon pepper
¼ teaspoon paprika

Spray a large skillet with butter-flavor nonstick cooking spray. Heat over medium heat until hot. Arrange the halibut steaks in a single layer in the prepared skillet. Cook for 3 to 4 minutes on each side. Add the white wine and lemon juice. Sprinkle the fillets with the basil, oregano, pepper and paprika. Simmer, covered, for 8 to 10 minutes or until the fish flakes easily. **Yield:** 4 servings.

PER SERVING:
CALORIES: 145; CARBOHYDRATE: 0.5 g; PROTEIN: 23.7 g; TOTAL FAT: 2.7 g;
CHOLESTEROL: 36 mg; SODIUM: 64 mg; FIBER: trace;
CALORIES FROM FAT: 17%

Pan-broiling using a nonstick skillet or nonstick cooking spray is a "legal" way to fry.

THE MAIN EVENT

Shrimp Jambalaya

1 tablespoon vegetable oil
1 tablespoon flour
1 cup chopped onion
1 cup chopped celery
1 cup chopped green bell pepper
4 ounces lower-salt lean ham, chopped
3 cloves of garlic, minced
2½ cups no-salt-added chicken broth
1 (14½-ounce) can no-salt-added whole tomatoes, chopped
¼ cup chopped fresh parsley
1 teaspoon thyme
½ teaspoon basil
¼ teaspoon black pepper
⅛ teaspoon ground red pepper
⅛ teaspoon salt
1 cup long grain rice
8 ounces medium shrimp, peeled, deveined

Spray a large nonstick skillet with nonstick cooking spray. Add the oil to the skillet. Stir in the flour. Cook over medium-high heat for 1½ minutes or until brown, stirring constantly. Add the onion, celery, green pepper, ham and garlic. Sauté for 7 minutes or until the vegetables are tender. Add the broth, undrained tomatoes, parsley, thyme, basil, black pepper, red pepper and salt. Bring to a boil. Add the rice and mix well; reduce heat. Simmer, covered, for 20 minutes or until the rice is tender. Stir in the shrimp. Cook, covered, for 5 minutes longer or until the shrimp turn pink, stirring occasionally.
Yield: 4 (1½-cup) servings.

Per Serving:
Calories: 356; Carbohydrate: 53 g; Protein: 20 g; Total Fat: 6 g;
Cholesterol: 79 mg; Sodium: 409 mg; Fiber: 3 g;
Calories from Fat: 16%

The Main Event

Lentil Burgers

1½ cups dry lentils
2½ cups water
1 medium onion, chopped
½ cup quick-cooking multi-grain oats
¼ cup egg substitute
¼ cup catsup
1 tablespoon hickory-flavor honey barbecue sauce
¼ teaspoon salt
⅛ teaspoon garlic powder
Lemon pepper to taste (optional)

Line a baking sheet with foil; spray with nonstick cooking spray or fat-free spray margarine. Sort and rinse the lentils. Combine the lentils and water in a heavy saucepan. Bring to a boil over medium-high heat; reduce heat. Simmer, covered, for 25 minutes; remove the cover. Simmer for 10 minutes longer or until the water is absorbed. Remove from heat. Stir in the onion, oats, egg substitute, catsup, barbecue sauce, salt, garlic powder and lemon pepper. Shape into 8 patties. Arrange on the prepared baking sheet. Chill for 1 hour or longer. Bake at 375 degrees for 20 to 25 minutes or until light brown. Serve on hamburger buns spread with fat-free mayonnaise and topped with sliced tomato, sliced onion, pickles and lettuce.
Yield: 8 servings.

Per Serving:
Calories: 154; Carbohydrate: 27.2 g; Protein: 10.6 g; Total Fat: 0.7 g;
Cholesterol: 0 mg; Sodium: 191 mg; Fiber: 3.8 g;
Calories from Fat: 4%

The Main Event

LAGNIAPPE

The word lagniappe has not yet passed into everyday use, but southerners instinctively understand the concept, if not the correct pronunciation.

For the record, it's pronounced "lan-yap" and the word is most familiar to inhabitants of the New Orleans region. The word comes to us from Louisiana French or Cajun, and derived originally from the Spanish term, la napa. It means "an extra, or unexpected gift: a gratuity."

So here's our unexpected gift to you—additional recipes for all types of foods that couldn't be neatly categorized in one of the other chapters of this book. As is usually the case with gifts, it's always more fun when they are totally unexpected and take you by surprise. We'd like to think that these recipes are surprising and that you'll have a lot of fun discovering them.

To borrow another Cajun phrase, "Laissez les bons temps roullez!," or let the good times roll!

*Cheekwood– Nashville's Home of Art and Gardens.
Inset: Cheekwood Mansion, built in 1929 as the private
residence of Mr. and Mrs. Leslie Cheek.*

CHITLINS

Clifton K. Meador, M.D.

Chitlins are in a class of food all by itself. So, before you run off to the market and buy fifteen or twenty feet of hog intestines, there are a few things you need to know. You don't cook chitlins on the spur of the moment.

The dictionary says "chitlins" or "chitlings" is a variation on "chitterlings." I think it is the other way around. In all your life have you ever heard anyone say "chitterling"? I haven't.

People in the South come in two forms. Those who eat chitlins, claim to like them, and even form clubs of chitlin-eaters. Then, there are the majority who have never tasted them and never will. I tasted them once. Trying to be polite, I made the mistake of telling a patient I would like to try some. He called my hand and showed up with a large serving. They looked like fried clams. I do not recall what they tasted like. He forced me to take a bite. The horror of what I was eating was so intense that I instantly fell unconscious and was left amnesic for the entire episode.

The truth is I took the chitlins home and fed them to my dog, who is inordinately fond of anything putrid. He ate the whole plateful and then wandered off in a daze. He ate nothing but grass for days afterwards.

John Edgerton, in his classic book "Southern Food," quotes Max Gergel of South Carolina: "You take a man and tie him to a stake and feed him bread and water for seven days and seven nights, and then he will eat a chitlin . . . He won't like it, but he will eat it."

That's enough background . . . on with the preparation and cooking. The only time to cook chitlins is in late November when it is cold and windy. John Edgerton quotes an old time chitlin cook as saying, "Lord, we'd never cook them things in the summertime. That smell would kill every green thing growing."

Getting the hog intestine clean must be the trick. Chitlin cooks say to turn the intestines inside out and scrape the lining real good. Of course you wash it many times. After you have washed and scraped, you turn the intestine so the inside is back inside. Then you cut lengths, say a couple of feet long and take three of the lengths and plait them together. After that, you take the two foot plaited lengths and put them in a large pot of boiling water and boil them until tender. When they are done, remove them and pat them with a towel. Now dredge them through flour and deep fat fry until crisp.

A friend of mine had a patient who claimed to be a chitlin expert. Asked if he really liked chitlins, the man answered, "Only if they're stump whipped and creek washed." Maybe that's the secret.

SPINACH CREAM CHEESE DIP

1 (10-ounce) package frozen chopped spinach, thawed, drained
8 ounces nonfat cream cheese, softened
¼ cup chopped radishes ♦ 2 tablespoons chopped green onions
1 tablespoon white wine ♦ ½ teaspoon garlic powder
¼ teaspoon pepper ♦ ¼ teaspoon tarragon ♦ ¼ teaspoon salt

Squeeze the moisture from the spinach. Combine the spinach, cream cheese, radishes, green onions, white wine, garlic powder, pepper, tarragon and salt in a bowl and mix well. Chill, covered, to enhance the flavor. Serve with low-fat butter crackers.
Yield: 28 (1-tablespoon) servings.

PER SERVING:
CALORIES: 10.4; CARBOHYDRATE: 1.0 g; PROTEIN: 1.3 g; TOTAL FAT: 0 g;
CHOLESTEROL: 5 mg; SODIUM: 72.5 mg; FIBER: trace;
CALORIES FROM FAT: 0%

CRANBERRY SALSA

12 ounces whole raw cranberries
1½ cups chopped green onions ♦ 2 tablespoons honey
2 tablespoons fresh lime juice ♦ 2 tablespoons fresh orange juice
2 tablespoons chopped fresh cilantro
1 tablespoon chopped fresh parsley
1 tablespoon tequila or dark rum (optional)
2 teaspoons minced seeded jalapeño ♦ ½ teaspoon pepper

Combine the cranberries, green onions, honey, lime juice, orange juice, cilantro, parsley, tequila, jalapeño and pepper in a food processor container. Process until of a chunky consistency.
Yield: 12 (2-tablespoon) servings.

PER SERVING:
CALORIES: 7.5; CARBOHYDRATE: 1.25 g; PROTEIN: 0 g; TOTAL FAT: 0 g;
CHOLESTEROL: 0 mg; SODIUM: 2.5 mg; FIBER: trace;
CALORIES FROM FAT: 0%

Avoid high-sodium foods such as cured meats, processed/pickled foods, condiments/seasoning salts/tenderizers, and snack foods.

LAGNIAPPE

171

Heart-Smart Croutons

Top any salad with these delicious croutons. To prepare the croutons, trim the crusts of your favorite sliced bread; spray both sides of the bread slices with nonstick cooking spray. Sprinkle with oregano, basil, thyme and garlic powder or any combination of your favorite herbs and spices. Toast in a 350-degree oven until light brown. Cut into ½-inch cubes.

Lagniappe

Light and Creamy Garlic Dressing

½ cup fat-free mayonnaise ♦ ½ cup plain nonfat yogurt
1 teaspoon chopped fresh parsley ♦ ⅛ teaspoon pepper
1 clove of garlic, minced ♦ 4½ teaspoons white wine vinegar
1 tablespoon Dijon mustard ♦ 1 tablespoon lemon juice

Combine the mayonnaise and yogurt in a bowl and mix well. Stir in the parsley, pepper and garlic. Whisk in the wine vinegar, Dijon mustard and lemon juice. Drizzle over your favorite green salad; top with Heart-Smart Croutons. Store in an airtight container in the refrigerator for up to 2 weeks. May substitute ½ teaspoon dried parsley flakes for the fresh parsley. **Yield:** 16 (1-tablespoon) servings.

Per Serving:
Calories: 9; Carbohydrate: 2 g; Protein: 0.5 g; Total Fat: 0 g;
Cholesterol: 0 mg; Sodium: 80 mg; Fiber: trace;
Calories from Fat: 0%

Chicken Gravy

1 cup low-sodium chicken broth
¼ cup skim milk ♦ 2 tablespoons flour
½ teaspoon freshly ground pepper, or to taste

Heat the broth in a saucepan over medium heat until warm. Combine the skim milk and flour in a jar with a tightfitting lid, shaking until blended. Add to the broth gradually, stirring constantly. Cook over medium heat until thickened, stirring constantly. Stir in the pepper; reduce heat. Cook for 5 minutes longer, stirring constantly. May substitute defatted chicken essence from the roasting pan for the low-sodium chicken broth. **Yield:** 16 (1-tablespoon) servings.

Per Serving:
Calories: 6; Carbohydrate: 1 g; Protein: 0 g; Total Fat: 0 g;
Cholesterol: 0 mg; Sodium: 6 mg; Fiber: trace;
Calories from Fat: 0%

QUICK AND EASY WHITE SAUCE

¼ cup plain nonfat yogurt
1 ounce Laughing Cow light cheese
2 tablespoons white wine
2 tablespoons low-fat low-sodium chicken broth
White pepper to taste

Combine the yogurt, cheese, white wine, broth and white pepper in a mixer bowl. Beat until smooth, scraping the bowl occasionally. Spoon into a microwave-safe dish. Microwave for 25 to 30 seconds or until heated through; do not boil. Try these quick and easy variations of the basic white sauce. For Alfredo Sauce, add ¼ cup grated fat-free Parmesan cheese, chopped fresh parsley, chopped fresh basil and ½ clove of minced garlic to the basic white sauce. For Mustard Sauce, add 1 tablespoon Dijon mustard to the basic white sauce. For Dill Sauce, add 1 tablespoon chopped fresh dillweed to the basic white sauce. For Herb Sauce, add 1 tablespoon of your favorite chopped fresh herbs to the basic white sauce. **Yield:** 2 (¼-cup) servings.

PER SERVING:
CALORIES: 51; CARBOHYDRATE: 2.7 g; PROTEIN: 4.2 g; TOTAL FAT: 1.5 g;
CHOLESTEROL: 5.6 mg; SODIUM: 210 mg; FIBER: trace;
CALORIES FROM FAT: 26%

LAGNIAPPE

CREAM OF BROCCOLI SOUP

1 (10-ounce) package frozen chopped broccoli
2 tablespoons reduced-calorie margarine
⅔ cup sliced fresh mushrooms
⅔ cup chopped onion
3 tablespoons flour
1 (12-ounce) can evaporated skim milk
¾ cup canned no-salt-added chicken broth
¼ teaspoon salt
¼ teaspoon whole thyme
¼ teaspoon pepper

Cook the broccoli using package directions; drain. Spray a large saucepan with nonstick cooking spray. Add the margarine to the prepared saucepan. Heat over medium heat until melted. Add the mushrooms and onion. Sauté until tender. Stir in the flour. Cook for 1 minute, stirring constantly. Add the evaporated skim milk and broth gradually and mix well. Cook until thickened, stirring constantly. Stir in the broccoli, salt, thyme and pepper. Cook until heated through, stirring frequently. Ladle into soup bowls.
Yield: 4 (1-cup) servings.

PER SERVING:
CALORIES: 155; CARBOHYDRATE: 20.2 g; PROTEIN: 10 g; TOTAL FAT: 4.6 g;
CHOLESTEROL: 3 mg; SODIUM: 345 mg; FIBER: 2.7 g;
CALORIES FROM FAT: 27%

LAGNIAPPE

Corn Chowder

1 cup chopped onion
6 cups (12 ears) fresh corn kernels with milk
3 cups chicken broth, skimmed
½ cup chopped red bell pepper
½ teaspoon chopped fresh rosemary
½ teaspoon thyme
⅛ teaspoon freshly ground black pepper
Cayenne to taste
1 tablespoon chopped fresh basil

Heat a large heavy saucepan over medium heat for 1 minute; spray twice with nonstick cooking spray. Sauté the onion in the prepared saucepan for 5 minutes or until tender. Add 4 cups of the corn. Sauté for 4 to 5 minutes or until tender. Add 2 cups of the broth and mix well. Cook for 20 minutes or until the corn mashes easily with a fork. Spoon the mixture into a blender container. Process until puréed. Return the purée to the saucepan. Stir in the remaining corn, remaining broth, red pepper, rosemary, thyme, black pepper and cayenne. Cook over medium-low heat for 10 minutes longer or until thick and creamy, stirring frequently. Ladle into soup bowls. Top each serving with fresh basil. **Yield:** 4 servings.

Per Serving:
Calories: 297; Carbohydrate: 66 g; Protein: 10.5 g; Total Fat: 3.9 g;
Cholesterol: 0 mg; Sodium: 80 mg; Fiber: 0.5 g;
Calories from Fat: 12%

Dietary fat intake should account for 30 percent or less of daily total calorie consumption.

Lagniappe

Spring Onion Soup

6 cups low-sodium chicken broth
¼ cup mixed dried morel and shiitake mushrooms
1 teaspoon olive oil
2 cups thinly sliced Vidalia onions
½ cup finely minced fresh sage
1 cup dry white wine
2 tablespoons minced fresh Italian parsley
Freshly ground pepper to taste

Heat 1 cup of the broth in a saucepan until hot. Pour over the mushrooms in a bowl. Let stand for 30 minutes. Drain, reserving the liquid. Mince the mushrooms. Heat the olive oil in a large stockpot. Add the onions and sage. Cook over low heat for 20 minutes or until the onion is tender, stirring frequently. Add the reserved liquid, mushrooms, remaining broth, white wine, parsley and pepper. Simmer, covered, for 40 minutes, stirring occasionally. Adjust the seasonings. Ladle into soup bowls. **Yield:** 4 servings.

Per Serving:
Calories: 78; Carbohydrate: 11 g; Protein: 3 g; Total Fat: 1 g;
Cholesterol: 0 mg; Sodium: 92 mg; Fiber: trace;
Calories from Fat: 22%

Lagniappe

Tangy Caesar Salad

2 garlic-flavor bagels
8 cups (1 large head) torn romaine
2 tablespoons freshly grated Parmesan cheese
1 teaspoon coarsely ground pepper
2 tablespoons lemon juice
2 teaspoons white wine Worcestershire sauce
1½ teaspoons red wine vinegar
½ teaspoon garlic powder
¼ teaspoon dry mustard
¼ cup plus 2 tablespoons plain nonfat yogurt

Cut each bagel horizontally into halves with a serrated knife. Cut each half horizontally into ¼-inch slices. Arrange on a baking sheet. Spray with butter-flavor nonstick cooking spray. Bake at 300 degrees for 25 minutes or until light brown and crisp. Combine the lettuce, cheese and pepper in a large salad bowl, tossing to mix. Combine the lemon juice, Worcestershire sauce, red wine vinegar, garlic powder and dry mustard in a small bowl and mix well. Stir in the yogurt. Pour over the lettuce mixture, tossing gently to coat. Break the bagel slices into small pieces. Add to the salad, tossing gently to mix. Serve immediately. May substitute 1 teaspoon minced fresh garlic for the garlic powder. **Yield:** 8 (1-cup) servings.

Per Serving:
Calories: 97; Carbohydrate: 16.6 g; Protein: 4.6 g; Total Fat: 1.3 g;
Cholesterol: 1 mg; Sodium: 186 mg; Fiber: trace;
Calories from Fat: 12%

Have salad dressing served beside your salad rather than on it, then dip your fork into it before placing a bite of salad into your mouth.

Lagniappe

177

SPINACH AND STRAWBERRY SALAD

1 tablespoon cornstarch
1 tablespoon sugar, or to taste
¼ teaspoon dry mustard
1 cup water
2½ tablespoons apple cider vinegar
2½ tablespoons honey
2 teaspoons poppy seeds
1½ teaspoons minced onion
¼ teaspoon Worcestershire sauce
¼ teaspoon paprika
2 bunches spinach, chilled, trimmed, torn into bite-size pieces
1 pint fresh strawberries, cut into halves

Combine the cornstarch, sugar and dry mustard in a saucepan and mix well. Stir in the water, cider vinegar and honey. Bring to a boil; reduce heat to medium. Cook until thickened, stirring constantly. Remove from heat. Cool slightly. Stir in the poppy seeds, onion, Worcestershire sauce and paprika. Chill, covered, until serving time. Combine the spinach and strawberries in a salad bowl just before serving, tossing gently to mix. Add the chilled dressing, tossing to coat. **Yield:** 8 servings.

PER SERVING:
CALORIES: 51; CARBOHYDRATE: 11 g; PROTEIN: 1 g; TOTAL FAT: trace;
CHOLESTEROL: 0 mg; SODIUM: 25 mg; FIBER: trace;
CALORIES FROM FAT: 10%

LAGNIAPPE

SCALLOPED POTATOES

2 tablespoons melted reduced-calorie margarine
2 tablespoons flour ♦ 2 cups skim milk
¼ teaspoon freshly ground pepper ♦ ⅛ teaspoon onion powder
⅛ teaspoon garlic powder
5 medium potatoes, peeled, thinly sliced ♦ ½ cup chopped onion

Mix the margarine and flour in a saucepan. Add the milk gradually, stirring constantly. Cook over medium heat until thickened. Stir in the pepper, onion powder and garlic powder. Arrange the potatoes and onion in the bottom of a 1½-quart baking dish sprayed with nonstick cooking spray. Pour the sauce over the top, stirring lightly. Bake, covered, at 350 degrees for 30 minutes; stir gently. Bake, uncovered, for 30 to 40 minutes or until tender. **Yield:** 5 servings.

PER SERVING:
CALORIES: 177; CARBOHYDRATE: 27 g; PROTEIN: 5 g; TOTAL FAT: 5.5 g;
CHOLESTEROL: 2 mg; SODIUM: 59 mg; FIBER: trace;
CALORIES FROM FAT: 28%

EASY ROSEMARY POTATOES

4 medium potatoes, peeled ♦ 1 tablespoon olive oil ♦ Salt to taste
1 teaspoon crushed rosemary ♦ ½ teaspoon garlic powder

Cut the potatoes into ⅜-inch slices. Cut the slices into ⅜-inch strips. Rinse in cold water. Drain and pat dry. Combine the olive oil, salt, rosemary and garlic powder in a large bowl and mix well. Add the potatoes, tossing to coat. Arrange the potatoes on an ungreased baking sheet. Bake at 425 degrees for 40 minutes or until the potatoes are brown and tender, stirring frequently. **Yield:** 4 servings.

PER SERVING:
CALORIES: 118; CARBOHYDRATE: 20 g; PROTEIN: 2.3 g; TOTAL FAT: 3.5 g;
CHOLESTEROL: 0 mg; SODIUM: 7 mg; FIBER: trace;
CALORIES FROM FAT: 27%

LAGNIAPPE

JALAPEÑO RICE

1⅓ cups water
⅔ cup long grain rice
1 cup cornmeal
½ teaspoon baking soda
½ teaspoon salt
1 cup skim milk
1 (8¾-ounce) can no-salt-added cream-style corn
½ cup chopped onion
½ cup frozen egg substitute, thawed
3 jalapeños, seeded, minced
1 tablespoon vegetable oil
¾ cup (3 ounces) shredded low-fat Monterey Jack cheese

Bring the water to a boil in a saucepan. Stir in the rice. Reduce heat. Simmer, covered, for 20 to 25 minutes or until the rice is tender and the liquid has been absorbed. Combine the cornmeal, baking soda and salt in a bowl and mix well. Stir in the rice, skim milk, corn, onion, egg substitute, jalapeños and oil. Spoon into a 7x11-inch baking dish sprayed with nonstick cooking spray. Bake at 350 degrees for 40 to 45 minutes or until golden brown. Sprinkle with the cheese. Bake for 5 minutes longer or until the cheese melts.
Yield: 12 servings.

PER SERVING:
CALORIES: 136; CARBOHYDRATE: 21.8 g; PROTEIN: 5.8 g; TOTAL FAT: 3.1 g;
CHOLESTEROL: 5 mg; SODIUM: 208 mg; FIBER: trace;
CALORIES FROM FAT: 20%

ACKNOWLEDGMENTS

Wilma Adams ◆ Renee Arbanas ◆ Kathy Amstutz
Laura Anderson ◆ Zil and JoAnn Athar ◆ Robert and Bessie Balch
Sam Barefield ◆ Helen Barry ◆ Sharon Bartleson
Joy Belton ◆ Chuck Bennett ◆ Helen Bergida
Madeline Biehler ◆ Denette Blankenship ◆ Gordon Bonnell
Irene Bradford ◆ Bob and Barbara Bundy ◆ Vivian Butkovich
Sandy Byrd ◆ Bart and Audrey Campbell
Wendy Chandler ◆ Donna Cheek ◆ Sarah Clark ◆ Mary Cummings
Jeanne Dalton ◆ Dianne Davenport ◆ Bobbie Davis
Ed and Roslynn Davis ◆ Al Delory ◆ Charles Ditmore
Carol Ellsworth ◆ Jodi Ervin ◆ Honey Foreman ◆ Susan Fussell
Stephanie Gibson ◆ Harold Goldberg
Rich Gordon ◆ Bill and Eleanor Gregory ◆ Gerry Hagan
Lois Hall ◆ Wendy Hall ◆ Mary Ann Harris ◆ Laurie Hays
Chef Richard Hoschar ◆ Lloyd and Marie Householder
Peggy Hutfilz ◆ Elaine Ihlenfeld ◆ Jane Jackson ◆ Betty James
Anna Johnson ◆ Bob Johnson ◆ Linda Jones ◆ Altha Keifer
Carolyn King ◆ Betty and Earl Kirshner ◆ Julie Kmet ◆ Aubrey Knott
Linda Lawrence ◆ Howard Liebowitz ◆ Bonita Lillie
Jimmy and Lillian Linn ◆ Laura Mangrum ◆ Randy March
George McAllister ◆ Bob and Georgiana McClenaghan
Kathy McDonagh ◆ Clifton K. Meador ◆ Martha Miller
Emma Mitchem ◆ Joni Morris ◆ Charles and Marian Nelson
Steve Newman ◆ Matt Norman ◆ Karin Waterman Oldham
Deborah Owens ◆ Paul Page ◆ Randy Pendergrass
Frank and Berta Perkins ◆ Cathey Powers ◆ Shara Randel
Danette Ranseen ◆ Johnny and Grace Reeves ◆ Connie Roberts
Susan Russell ◆ Roya Saeedpour ◆ Mark Sloan ◆ Doug Smith
Annie Starnes ◆ John Tighe ◆ Travis Tjepkema ◆ Janice Vantrease
Peggy Wampler ◆ Mary Watson ◆ Cathy Welsh ◆ Kim Wilhelm
Dick and Helen Williams ◆ Patsy and Hy Wind
Gwen Wood

NUTRITIONAL PROFILE GUIDELINES

The recipes in this cookbook were analyzed by, or under the direction of, a registered dietitian. This cookbook is for any individual wishing to make lifestyle changes to reduce the risk of heart disease. The collection of recipes have been modified to reduce total fat, saturated fat, cholesterol, and sodium. Persons who have diabetes mellitus may use these recipes if they are using the carbohydrate counting method of the American Diabetic Association exchange system; however, recipes containing excessive simple carbohydrates and sugars are not suitable. References used for analysis include *Bowes and Church's Food Values of Portions Commonly Used*, by Jean A. T. Pennington, 15th and 16th editions, and available nutrition information from newly released food products. All of the recipes are 30% or less calories from fat, less than 10% of calories from saturated fat, 300 mg. or less cholesterol, and sodium under 3,000 mg. per day as recommended by the National Cholesterol Education Program and the American Heart Association. Persons with dietary or health problems, whose diets require close monitoring, should consult their physician or registered dietitian for specific information.

♦ Alcoholic ingredients have been analyzed for the basic ingredients, although cooking causes the evaporation of alcohol, thus decreasing caloric content.

♦ Buttermilk, sour cream and yogurt are the types available commercially which contain 1% milkfat or less.

♦ Cottage cheese is 1% milkfat or nonfat.

♦ Cheese is reduced-fat containing 5 grams fat or less per one-ounce portion, or fat-free.

♦ Milk is 1% milkfat, ½% milkfat or skim. Evaporated milk is skimmed evaporated milk, and sweetened condensed milk is the fat-free type.

♦ Flour is unsifted all-purpose unless the recipe specifies unbleached, self-rising, whole wheat, etc.

♦ Margarine is the type containing liquid oil as its first ingredient.

♦ Oil is either canola or olive oil unless specified otherwise.

♦ Chicken, cooked for boning and chopping, has been roasted; this method yields the lowest caloric value.

♦ Egg white is the white of 1 large egg, and eggs when used are large. Cholesterol-free egg substitutes are the varieties with ¼ cup equivalent to 1 egg.

♦ Salt and other ingredients to taste as noted in the ingredients have not been included in the nutritional profile.

♦ Garnishes, serving suggestions, and other optional additions and variations are not included in the profile.

♦ If a choice of ingredients has been given, the nutritional profile information reflects the first option. If a choice of amounts has been given, the nutritional profile reflects the greater amount.

RECIPE INGREDIENT GUIDE

When your recipe calls for:	*Available products
Low-fat pasteurized process cheese	Kraft® Velveeta Light®
Low-fat cheese	Cheese containing <5 grams fat per 1-ounce portion
Low-fat butter-type crackers	SnackWell's® Golden Classic Crackers
Butter-flavor nonstick cooking spray	Weight Watcher's® Buttery Spray
Fat-free spray margarine	I Can't Believe It's Not Butter!® Spray
Butter-flavor sprinkles	Butter Buds®; Molly McButter®
Liquid butter-flavor sprinkles	Butter Buds®; follow mixing directions on box
Acceptable margarine	Margarine with first ingredient: Liquid oil
Olive oil-flavor nonstick cooking spray	Olive Oil Pam® No Stick Cooking Spray
Chocolate wafers	Nabisco® Famous Chocolate Wafers
Light cream cheese	Kraft® Philadelphia® ⅓ Less Fat (block); Kraft® Philadelphia® Light™ (tub)
Nonfat cream cheese or fat-free cream cheese	Kraft® Philadelphia® Free®; Healthy Choice®; Healthy Indulgence™
Low-sodium chicken or beef bouillon	Wyler's® LOW-SODIUM Instant Bouillon; Herb-Ox® VERY LOW-SODIUM INSTANT BROTH AND SEASONING
Low-sodium canned chicken broth	Campbell's® Low-Sodium CHICKEN BROTH
Lower-salt, lean ham	Smithfield 33⅓% Lower-Sodium Ham
Low-sodium soy sauce	Angostura® Soy Sauce

*We are not claiming to endorse these products. Other brands with nutrient similarities may be used as well.

KITCHEN AND PANTRY BASICS

Cooking and Baking Products

Assorted fresh/dried herbs and
  spices
Mrs. Dash/sodium-free
  herb/spice blends
Butter Buds
Cholesterol-free egg substitute
Garlic powder
Onion powder
Black pepper
Red pepper
Salt/light salt/salt substitute
Molly McButter
Soy bacon bits
Baking cocoa
Nonfat dry milk
Canola oil
Olive oil
Nonstick cooking spray
  (original, butter-flavor, olive
  oil-flavor)
Margarine with first ingredient
  liquid oil

Vegetables

Canned, no salt added
Frozen-plain
Fresh, when available
Tomato sauce, no salt added
Canned/stewed tomatoes,
  no salt added
Tomato paste, no salt
  added

Condiments

Reduced-calorie mayonnaise
Fat-free mayonnaise
Fat-free salad dressings
Mustard, all varieties
Catsup
Liquid Smoke
White wine Worcestershire sauce
Worcestershire sauce
Vinegar, all varieties
Commercial spaghetti sauce,
  sodium reduced (less than
  4 grams fat per 4 ounces)
Tabasco/hot sauce
Sweet pickle relish
Fresh salsa/no-salt-added salsa
Low-sodium soy sauce

Breads, Grains, Cereals, Desserts, Snacks

Cholesterol-free pasta
No-yolk noodles
Brown rice
Quick-cooking rice
Oatmeal
Oat bran
All-Bran
Bran buds
100% bran
Melba toast
Unsalted top saltines
Low-fat/fat-free snack crackers,
  i.e., SnackWells by Nabisco

Breads, Grains, Cereals,
   Desserts, Snacks (continued)
Vanilla wafers
Graham crackers
Gingersnaps
Newton-type cookies
Angel food cake
Low-fat, low-salt popcorn
Unsalted/sodium-reduced
   pretzels
Baked nacho chips,
   unsalted/lightly salted
Baked potato chips, unsalted/
   lightly salted
Fat-free commercial dips
English muffins
Fat-free tortillas
Pita bread
Bagels
French/Italian bread

Milk and Dairy Products
Buttermilk (1% milkfat or less)
Skim milk
½% milk
1% milk

Light or fat-free cream cheese
Light or nonfat sour cream
1% milkfat or nonfat yogurts
Reduced-fat or skim/part-skim
   cheeses (5 grams fat/
   1-ounce portion)
Skimmed evaporated milk
   1% milkfat/fat-free frozen
   dessert (ice milk, etc.)
Low-fat/nonfat frozen yogurt
Sherbet
Sorbet
Fat-free cheese, all varieties
Fat-free Parmesan cheese
Puddings made with skim milk

Miscellaneous
Reduced-sodium canned beef
   broth
Reduced-sodium canned chicken
   broth
Low-sodium beef and chicken
   bouillon
Reduced-fat/reduced-salt soups
Water-pack low-salt tuna
Natural peanut butter

Season with Care

- Dried herbs stored in the freezer will keep much longer.
- To use fresh herbs in a recipe that calls for dried, triple the amount specified.
- Herbs and spices should be kept in a cool, dry place away from the sun and stove.
- To supply a salty taste, try dehydrated onion flakes or onion powder, lemon juice, garlic flakes or powder, celery seeds, parsley, or hot pepper sauce.
- Seasonings for fish include: allspice, basil, bay leaves, caraway seeds, cayenne, celery seeds, chives, cilantro, curry, dillweed, garlic, ginger, herbed vinegars, lemon, lime, mace, marjoram, mint, onion, orange, oregano, paprika, parsley, rosemary, saffron, sage, tarragon, and thyme.
- Seasonings and flavors for pork include: apple cider, black beans, brown sugar, caraway seeds, cardamom, cilantro, cloves, dill, garlic, ginger, honey, jalapeños, lemon and orange marmalade, molasses, onion, red wine vinegar, rosemary, saffron, sage, tarragon, and thyme.
- Great toppings for air-popped popcorn include: garlic powder, chili powder, cayenne, onion powder, Parmesan cheese, salt-free seasonings, or curry powder.
- Add salt substitute after the food is cooked because cooking with a salt substitute will make the food taste bitter.
- When using a salt substitute, shake on gently, because a little goes a long way.
- Steam, microwave, or sauté vegetables in broth or flavored vinegars. Enhance the flavor with lemon juice, herbs, and spices.

SUBSTITUTIONS

Recipe Indicates:	*Use Instead:*
1 cup sugar	¾ cup sugar
1 cup walnuts	½ cup walnuts
½ cup oil, margarine or butter (in baking)	½ cup applesauce
	¼ cup applesauce and ¼ cup buttermilk
	½ cup baby food prunes (in chocolate recipes)
½ cup oil (in marinades, salad dressings)	½ cup pineapple juice
½ cup margarine, butter (for icings)	½ cup marshmallow creme
	½ cup fat-free tub margarine
2 tablespoons oil (for sautéing)	2 tablespoons defatted broth
	2 tablespoons unsweetened pineapple juice
	2 tablespoons dry wine
1 cup heavy cream	1 cup evaporated skim milk
1 cup sour cream	1 cup plain nonfat yogurt
	1 cup puréed nonfat cottage cheese and 1 tablespoon lemon juice
	1 cup nonfat sour cream
1 whole egg	2 egg whites
	¼ cup cholesterol-free egg substitute
Whipped cream (on fruit, desserts)	nonfat or low-fat vanilla yogurt
Cream (in coffee)	Skim milk
	Powdered nonfat dry milk
Butter or margarine (on potatoes or other vegetables)	Butter Buds, liquid or dry
	Molly McButter
1 cup whole milk	1 cup skim milk, ½% or 1% milk
1 cup whole milk yogurt	1 cup skim milk yogurt
Salad dressing	Yogurt, mixed with lemon, vinegar, herbs and spices, or oil-free dressing
1 cup creamed cottage cheese	1 cup nonfat cottage cheese
Cheese made from whole milk or cream	Cheese made from skim milk or part skim milk
	Cheese containing less than 5 grams of fat per 1-ounce portion

Recipe Index

Photograph Index